A Short History of the
American Stomach

"Who knew that Cotton Mather was America's first food faddist or Benjamin Franklin our founding foodie? I loved every chapter of Kaufman's book. American history has never been so much fun."

— MARION NESTLE, author of *What to Eat*

"*A Short History of the American Stomach* gives us something fresh, mixing erudition and passion with a tempered, lean, accurate prose that never misses its beats and never compromises a witty economy of style. Petronius would be proud."

— LAWRENCE OSBORNE, author of
The Accidental Connoisseur

"Kaufman makes brilliant use of humor and history to expose Americans' bipolar relationship with food. This is the book to read if you want to understand why, generation after generation, we doggedly persist in dividing edibles into good and bad, healthy and deadly, alternately stuffing then depriving ourselves, worshiping processed foods one year and organic the next, ad nauseam."

— BARRY GLASSNER, author of *The Gospel of Food*

"Fred Kaufman's rollicking tour of America's gastronomic tract is part history, part travelogue, and part cultural meditation. The story he tells is engaging, literate, and often hilariously weird, a bracing combination of Marco Polo and Julia Child, mingled together with a spicy dash of Ambrose Bierce."

— ADAM PLATT, *New York* magazine food critic

"With dazzling erudition and wit, Frederick Kaufman illuminates America's vexed obsession with eating (and non-eating) from Puritan times to the present. This is journalistic history at its best."
— DAVID S. REYNOLDS, author of
Waking Giant: America in the Age of Jackson

"Funny, erudite, and wise, Frederick Kaufman's romp through the dark recesses of America's culinary obsessions astonishes and enlightens at every turn."
— MICHAEL GREENBERG,
author of *Hurry Down Sunshine*

"Kaufman's witty historical analysis will be a treat for anyone interested in food."
— *Time Out New York*

"Kaufman covers a lot of ground, but he does it with sly verbal chicanery and wit."
— *Deseret Morning News*

"Americans' penchant to binge and purge, to regularly visit the extremes of eating and dieting, has a long and noble history. Kaufman nimbly chronicles this endless cycle of excess and deprivation."
— *Booklist*

"Kaufman . . . pursues a hip, journalistic approach to America's all-consuming relationship to the gut, from Puritan rituals of fasting to the creation of the Food Network . . . [An] entertaining study."
— *Publishers Weekly*

"A series of trenchant arguments about the consistency of Americans' feelings for food, our great common denominator . . . Kaufman's jolting chapter on vomiting (he prefers 'puking') displays a masterful wit . . . Gourmets and gourmands alike will savor Kaufman's keen, caustic anatomy of the American palate."
— *Kirkus Reviews*

A Short History of the
American Stomach

A Short History
of the
American
Stomach

Frederick Kaufman

MARINER BOOKS • HOUGHTON MIFFLIN HARCOURT   Boston   New York

First Mariner Books edition 2009
Copyright © 2008 by Frederick Leonard Kaufman

For information about permission to reproduce selections from this book,
write to Permissions, Houghton Mifflin Harcourt Publishing Company,
6277 Sea Harbor Drive, Orlando, Florida 32887-6777.

www.hmhbooks.com

Versions of "Debbie Does Salad" and "The Secret Ingredient" were
published in *Harper's*, and material from two other *Harper's* articles,
'Fat of the Land" and "Our Daily Bread," is incorporated into this book
in different form. Also, material from a *New Yorker* "Talk of the Town"
piece called "Psst! Got Milk?" is incorporated into this book.

Library of Congress Cataloging-in-Publication Data
Kaufman, Frederick, date.
A short history of the American stomach/Frederick Kaufman.—1st ed.
p.   cm.
Includes index.
1. Stomach—Social aspects.   2. Stomach—History.   3. Food habits—
United States—History.   4. United States—Social life and customs.
I. Title.
GT498.S76K48   2008
394.1'2—dc22   2007017282
ISBN 978-0-15-101194-0
ISBN 978-0-15-603469-2 (pbk.)

Text set in Goudy Old Style MT
Designed by April Ward

Printed in the United States of America

BTA 10 9 8 7 6 5 4 3 2 1

for Phoebe and Julian
and for Lizzie

CONTENTS

PREFACE

The Council taking into their serious consideration the low estate of the churches of God throughout the world, and the increase of sin and evil amongst ourselves, God's hand following us for the same, do therefore appoint the two and twentieth of this instant September to be a Day of Publick Humiliation.

—Boston proclamation, 1670

The American Institute of Wine and Food had sponsored the "Food & Fiction" workshop, and it was all very cozy and quite literary. The audience understood the basic idea: America had to reject the commercialization of our food stream; we had to return to natural ingredients; we had to support the economics of family farms; we had to appreciate the latent spirituality of our appetites; we had to embrace the poetry of garlic and cilantro and capers and okra. My fellow panelists read their studiously crafted paragraphs about epicureanism, alimentum, and heirloom tomatoes. Then it was my turn, and as I detailed the history of Puritan puking practices, the foodies sat in horror.

During the question-and-answer period, a young woman in the back raised her hand.

"This is a question for Kaufman," she said. "Why are you writing about vomit?"

As far back as I could remember writing seriously about anything, I had been writing about the relationship between the mind and the body—with an emphasis on the gut. A college essay about *The Odyssey* became an analysis of the hero and the stomach, particularly those stomachs that wanted to digest the hero. "Demented," the professor had scribbled.

Years later I found myself at a cocktail party and happened into Lewis Lapham, who at the time was the editor of *Harper's Magazine.* I pitched an article about American gastrosophy. "What's that?" he asked.

Gastrosophy had been the name for the physiological, psychological, and philosophical study of the stomach, a discipline that had reached a zenith of sorts in early nineteenth-century America. Lapham gave me a searching look. The minute details of American heartburn in the 1820s, fascinating as they might have been to me, would not merit a contract with his magazine. So I added a new angle to the pitch, something that had not occurred to me until that desperate moment.

"It's an article about the diet-book mania today and how it compares to the diet-book mania a hundred and fifty years ago."

"There was a diet-book mania a hundred and fifty years ago?" he asked.

Harper's did eventually assign the article, and I was soon delving deep into the bloated underbelly of our history. There I discovered ever more monstrous troves of food fads, food taboos, food fetishes, and paranoias regarding what would or would not pass the threshold of our lips. Eating too much was hardly a new national development, nor was eating too little, nor was our endless search for the cures. And the more I learned, the more convinced I became that absolutely nothing had changed.

What if a single historical thread spun from Rachael Ray all the way back to that cold morning when the first famished Pilgrim clambered off the *Mayflower*? And what if that thread were our intestine? Perhaps the entrails branched wider and deeper than anyone had ever imagined.

There was no evading the conclusion: Contrary to popular opinion, neither American overeating nor American refusal to eat was the creation of postwar plenty, of overstressed adolescents, or of McDonald's. The feast and the fast have always been American twins: anorexia and obesity, binge and purge, pollution and purity, the mania of stuffing everything into our imperial system and our sober insistence on solitude, separation, and perfect self-reliance. From the first ordained fast days of Salem and Plymouth to the latest wave of not eating as detox alternative therapy, the United States was and remains one of the most gut-centric and gut-phobic societies in the history of human civilization.

But in order to understand this country's ever-growing phalanx of raw-food enthusiasts, and in order to account for kosher Snickers bars and soapy food-TV hostesses who pose for magazines thigh-deep in sinks of dishwater; in order to grasp the glut of food blogs, fruitarian Web sites, kitchen.coms, bestselling books about salt and coffee and cod, and special food issues of the *New Yorker*, the *Nation*, and the *New York Times Book Review*; in order to render intelligible the countless millions of dollars spent each month on kitchen renovations, on food vacations, and on food retreats to Aspen and Sonoma; in order to penetrate the industry's endless quest for the next big flavor, be it leather, oak, seawater foam, or mousse that savors of the earth; and in order to fathom the food scares and art lettuces, the *Rosengarten Reports* and gubernatorial campaigns that hinge on the horrors and seductions of un-American shellfish—we must follow the winding road of the American intestine back to its famished origins. Only here might we find the origins of the strange belief that anyone with enough savvy and discipline can satisfy his or her appetite, no matter how gigantic. A belief otherwise known as the American Dream.

There are those who take exception to exceptionalism, the chauvinistic notion that there could be such a thing as a particularly American anything, much less an Americanized interior organ. But few would argue with the basic assertion that America was originally an idea; and fewer still would dispute that this idea has steadily grown more pervasive. Call it what you will: globalization, Western culture, the Global North, hegemony, imperialism. Like our waistlines, it's expanding.

The stomach lies at the center of this American idea. Our understanding of virtue and vice, success and failure, has long been expressed in the language of appetite, consumption, and digestion. In America a carrot is never just a carrot. As she faced the aftermath of a civil war that had brought more carnage to the country than any conflict before or since, Catharine Beecher flatly stated, "It is the opinion of most medical men, that intemperance in eating is one of the most fruitful of all causes of disease and death." Catharine and her sister (Harriet Beecher Stowe, who was as well-known as a diet reformer as for *Uncle Tom's Cabin*), would have nodded approvingly at the recent declaration of Dr. Kelly Brownell, chair of Yale's Psychology Department and of its Center for Eating and Weight Disorders, that America is a "toxic food environment," in which "we are literally eating ourselves to death." A potato sizzling in grease was a moral, ethical, and political issue to the Beechers, as evil as soda in schools today.

The Puritans, who believed that the perfections

and pollutions of the stomach reflected an individual's spiritual state, laid the groundwork by injecting moral content into everything they would or would not eat. The doctors of the time confirmed the centrality of the stomach—they understood the gut to be the element that regulated everything else within the human body. With medical and spiritual guidelines in place, it was only a matter of time before eating—what, when, and how much—became a means of social control. Could the fixation on the stomach's health and turmoil (and the host of violent remedies visited on the suffering organ) have influenced the American Revolution's fixation on the political health and turmoil of the body politic? Was it merely a coincidence that the birth of an independent constitution correlated with the momentary triumph of the study of the stomach over and above all other medical disciplines? Was our new nation the gut's greatest victory?

The post-Revolutionary remains of stomach science grew to flourish in nineteenth-century America. The digestive tract entered the poetry of Walt Whitman, the fiction of Nathaniel Hawthorne and Herman Melville, and the prose of Emerson and Thoreau. Transcendentalist tracts advocated a "natural" diet of roots and berries, while Gilded Age gastrophiles gulped oysters and champagne. Voluminous cookbooks and even more voluminous tomes of dietary inquiry became publishing successes. And the gut drove Americans to the frontier.

But just as the Americans devoured their land with a level of deliberation and violence hitherto unknown, they also created a new one to consume. What was our vaunted optimism but the gut's will to power? If and when we've eaten all that the world has to offer, we'll simply cook up a fresh one, a cosmos commensurate to our appetites. In 1803 a Maryland butter merchant named Thomas Moore invented the refrigerator. In 1854 a chemist named Eben Horsford synthesized baking powder. In 1879 a Johns Hopkins University professor named Ira Remsen experimented with a coal tar compound and found it possessed a sweetening power roughly five hundred times that of cane sugar. It was saccharin. From the USDA's Western Wheat Quality Laboratory recently emerged an extra-pasty, polymer-addled cereal called Penawawa-X—which will guarantee very satisfying flat bread and udon just in case we ever lose our taste for Wonder and whole grain.

Whether Puritan refusal or Wild West voraciousness reigns, the rule of the stomach will endure; we can go with our gut or try to suppress it, but it is always running the show. The American stomach seeks nothing less than to create the earth anew, and this country—ever eager to consume, ever eager to deny, so fixated on the shape of its individual bodies, so mesmerized by and so oblivious to the provenance of its food—this country will persist in its obsessions until it digests the world.

Debbie Does Salad

A modern epicure is almost always eating the present dish as a kind of introduction to something else.
—William Alcott, 1846

In the year 2000 an American Cinco de Mayo celebration featured the world's largest taco, fashioned from nine hundred pounds of meat. The taco generated a fair bit of press but could not compare to the sensation created almost two hundred years earlier when supporters of Thomas Jefferson presented the president with a New Year's gift, a nine-hundred-pound "Mammoth Cheese," said to have been produced from the milk of one thousand Republican cows. Such tales amuse but don't amaze us anymore. The outrageous demands of the American stomach have become our daily bread.

But back in the day when Federalists walked the earth, the stomach could still engender shock and awe. In January of 1803, not too long after the presentation of that mammoth cheese, a young journalist who called himself Jonathan Oldstyle traversed the most fashionable streets of New York City, astonished by the extraordinary abundance of food, and by the extraordinary might of its consumption. He published his cultural observations in New York's *Morning Chronicle*:

> I had marched into the theatre through rows of tables heaped up with delicacies of every kind—here a pyramid of apples or oranges invited the playful palate of the dainty; while there a regiment of mince pies and custards promised a more substantial regale to the hungry. I entered the box, and looked around with astonishment . . . The crackling of nuts and the crunching of apples saluted my ears on every side. Surely, thought I, never was an employment followed up with more assiduity than that of gormandizing; already it pervades every public place of amusement . . .
>
> The eating mania prevails through every class of society; not a soul but has caught the infection. Eating clubs are established in every street and alley, and it is impossible to turn a corner without hearing the hissing of frying pans, winding the savory steams of roast and boiled, or seeing some hungry genius bolting raw oysters in the middle of the street.

Within a decade, this young food writer would become America's most famous author. His name was Washington Irving.

Irving was a social critic, and his food writing, social commentary. In an 1807 edition of *Salmagundi* (a literary magazine he founded with his brother and a friend), Irving declared that

> the barbarous nations of antiquity immolated human victims to the memory of their lamented dead, but the enlightened Americans offer up whole hecatombs of geese and calves, and oceans of wine in honour of the illustrious living . . .

Irving had perceived that eating and drinking in the pristine nation introduced an entirely new set of rituals and sacraments, for food and food alone could embody "the sublime spectacle of love of country, elevating itself from a sentiment into an appetite."

A few decades after Irving's magazine pieces, the obsessions of nineteenth-century food maniacs had matured from raw oysters, raw apples, and nuts into the liver puddings and chicken jellies of Miss Eliza Leslie's *Directions for Cookery*. The most popular cookbook of the nineteenth century, *Directions* plowed its way through sixty printings, sold hundreds of thousands of copies, and made its author one of the first in a long line of celebrity chefs. And Miss Leslie, famous for her sarcasm and wit, grew so expansive that in her final years she could not walk.

A century and a half before the advent of Zagat online and starchefs.com, American food delirium had already engendered a sect of haute-bourgeois extravagance—our first clearly recognizable foodies (as opposed to the chowhounds, who had been gnawing bark off the trees from the very beginning). Hard-line nineteenth-century food moralists such as Sylvester Graham and William Alcott may have railed against the immoral luxuries of white bread, store-bought milk, and more than two ingredients per dish, but Jacksonian gastrosophisticates continued to lust after Miss Leslie's peach leather and gooseberry fool, cocoa-nut pudding, and raspberry charlotte. The food protestants knew that beneath such culinary desires lay perversity, sickness, and damnation, but their rhetoric could hardly diminish the popularity of America's first haunt of high cuisine, the restaurant Delmonico's, where the menu featured chateaubriand, lobster Newburg, and limitless liters of Château Margaux. With dread imagination, the reformers could envision a marketplace glutted with disease-inducing excitements (i.e., spices) and chemically tainted butter. Never could they have conceived of our present debauched trade in chocolate fountains and olive stoners, thermoforks, ergonomic meat hammers, and bidirectional marinade injectors.

America's eating infection has progressed, just as our obsessive need to possess recipes has morphed from shoe boxes stuffed with file cards to cookbooks .com, a database that brims with one million possibilities. To sample every one of them (at a steady rate of three meals per day, one new recipe per meal) would take more than nine hundred years.

But don't be absurd. Nobody cooks all those recipes. In fact, everyone knows recipes aren't for cooking. Instead, the relationship of the recipe to the typical American cook has transformed into something akin to the relationship between sexual intercourse and the voyeur. So, after you've exhausted the offerings from cookbooks.com (which should take a week or so), the more traditional style of cookbook awaits—the profusion of which has managed to dwarf the diet-book industry. More than thirty-nine thousand inheritors of Miss Leslie's tradition account for business worth $375 million a year. The books fall into the classic divisions, the clinical manifestations of American food mania: imperialist (*Superfoods, How to Cook Everything, The Whole Beast: Nose to Tail Eating*); scientific (*Molecular Gastronomy, What Einstein Told His Cook*); spiritual (*The Sauce Bible, The Smoothies Bible, The Bread Bible, The Pie and Pastry Bible*, along with innumerable barbecue, wine, and mixed-drink bibles); and medical (*The Self-Healing Cookbook, The Fibromyalgia Cookbook, The Dysphagia Cookbook*).

And then there are the hordes of recipe monomaniacs, ready to plunk down ducats for single-titled tomes devoted entirely to eggs or cheese, cupcakes or crepes, dough or salmon. (Not to neglect fried chicken, apple pie, or *The Book of Yogurt*.) Scores of sexually suggestive offerings mix and match involuntary impulses (*Saucepans and the Single Girl*; *Dining in the Raw*; *InterCourses*; *Fork Me, Spoon Me*). Add to the above an entire sector of the business that has developed around treatises expressly dedicated to cooking equipment—from convection ovens and microwaves to woks, juicers, food processors, pressure cookers, rice cookers, slow cookers, and the tagine. Not to mention the thousands upon thousands of ecstatic pages devoted to the grill, George Foreman and otherwise. Vegetarian tracts have laid waste the forests.

Peculiar cookbooks demand peculiar ingredients. Just as the postmodern intestinal devotee (someone like you, dear reader) can order vinegar six-packs from eBay, loquat vinegar from igourmet.com, and chocolate vinegar from cybercucina.com, Miss Leslie provided meticulous instructions for the creation of such gastronomic wonders as shallot vinegar, chili vinegar, and horseradish vinegar—the last of which none of the sites presently carries. While many of us have moved beyond the specifics of Miss Leslie's oatmeal gruel and rennet whey, our eating mania has persevered. Inundated as we are with shelf loads of champagne honey mustards, cognac quince mustards, and handcrafted carmelized ginger-fig mustards (not to mention ever-growing stockpiles of mango, watermelon, and star-fruit chutneys), we hardly note that in the great tradition of American food madness, we are worshipping at the altar of the edible.

If and when we ever stop to think about our need for that perfect fennel wasabi habanero, we consider our yearning an outgrowth of modern, international, sophisticated tastes honed in the decades since Julia Child introduced us to aspic. We take our nori-wrapped artisanal foie gras, our roasted cilantro shisho chiffonades, and our tikka masala tapenades as signs of our contemporary culture of epicureanism. It certainly never occurs to us that when it comes to our stomachs, we long ago lost all capacity for reason.

That's because our stomachs aren't governed by reason. Recent scientific investigations have led to increasingly refined theories of the stomach's power. American researchers have disinterred a medical theory from more than a century ago that places the stomach in the center of everything, a theory that asserts the digestive tract constitutes a brain in and of itself. "Gut reaction" has become more than a phrase.

Michael Gershon, chairman of Columbia University's Department of Anatomy and Cell Biology, believes there is a brain in the gut. This "second brain" has a hundred million neurons—which is more than the spinal cord—and controls the expansion and contraction of the body's sphincters, the

O-ring muscles located, among other places, up and down the digestive tract. Any elementary human-biology textbook will tell you there are sphincters in the pupils of the eyes, sphincters in the heart, and sphincters in the sexual organs. There are cervical sphincters, urethral sphincters, pyloric sphincters, two separate and distinct anal sphincters, and the sphincter of Oddi, which controls secretions from the liver, pancreas, and gallbladder. But we never have to think much about getting food from our throats to our stomachs, from our stomachs to our intestines, and from our intestines on down, just as we don't have to calculate how to equilibrate our own blood pressure. According to Professor Gershon, the brain in the gut takes care of such things.

Of course, Michael Gershon was not the first American scientist to reach such conclusions. Frederick Byron Robinson's landmark study "The Abdominal Brain and Pelvic Brain" was first published in Chicago in 1907. "In the abdomen there exists a brain of wonderful power maintaining eternal, restless vigilance over its viscera," wrote Robinson.

> It presides over organic life. . . . It is the center of life itself. . . . The abdominal brain can live without the cranial brain, which is demonstrated by living children being born without cerebrospinal axis. On the contrary the cranial brain can not live without the abdominal brain.

Even when we sleep, the web of nervous plexuses emanating from that ancient region of the visceral brain remains awake.

Most places on earth, this brain in the gut remains secondary: technical support for the plot, character, and action of daily life. Only in America have the viscera been put in charge. The primeval brain of the involuntary, the abdominal brain, the autonomic brain that controls sympathy and revulsion but not rationality—that is the brain of the American stomach. Our gut has a mind of its own, and that mind is our mind.

It was only a matter of time before the information age, with its manifold digital and broadband technologies, would bow down before the stomach. And so our abiding reverence for the digestive—the long-standing American romance with gut reaction—has impelled cash-bloated cable executives to strategize an explosive diversification of the food television market over the next ten years. Soon we can expect the Food Network Italian, the Food Network Southern, the Gourmet Food Channel, the Food and Wine Channel, the Jewish Food Channel, the California Food Channel, and more. For just as food TV marks a culmination of sorts in the history of American food fervor, it also marks a beginning.

I began to watch the Food Network after my editor casually mentioned that she believed food media deserved a place of honor in a history of the American stomach, and soon I was sitting for hours in front of the tube, pretending I was in the midst of a grave and extensive research project. I would head to the kitchen during commercials, stock up on potato chips and caffeine, then settle back for the next show. Orecchiette with turkey sausage, seared rib-eye steak with arugula and roasted-pepper salad, chocolate zabaglione . . .

Truth was I had become an addict. I couldn't wait for Emeril to show me his banana quesadillas, or Rachael Ray to whip up her next batch of sloppy joe. It seemed as though they were cooking just for me. Late into the night I sat mesmerized by *Unwrapped*, the behind-the-scenes-at-the-food-factory half hour featuring the thrum of conveyor belts, the shimmer of food robots, the glow of 240-foot hell-on-earth ovens, and the strange beauty of extrusion. I have vivid recollections of an immense contrivance that coated a thousand pretzels with sodium hydroxide, and one particular episode of *Top 5* called "Sugary Seductions": lush images of caramel and apple and chocolate and pecan, swirling to a salsa beat.

I gaped at airbrushed flowers made of gum paste, chocolate DVDs, gummy watches, edible cell phones, and sparkling glucose dinnerware manufactured by someone who called himself the "Marquis de Sweet." I watched segments devoted to dough-nut dreams, chocolate fantasies, and the world's stickiest foods. I can still hear that syrupy voice-over: "We've got some of the hottest innovations in candyland . . ."

"Taste life" has long been one of the Food Network's mottoes—as though watching TV somehow constituted life more lifelike than life itself. As though the actual flour and sugar and carrots and onions, in their most recent incarnation as glittering objects of delight and desire, had not devolved into airtime and advertising dollars and vanished into the commodified ether. Some people suffering from bulimia have referred to their disorder as "angelic eating," because you get the sensual thrill of food without the bodily trace. Was food TV like angelic eating or some other metaphor even more subversive, a metaphor that still eluded me?

We all know that cooking on camera experienced its first hit with Julia Child on Boston public television, but attained its present commercial status only in the last decade of the twentieth century. To be specific, the postmodern age of food media began in 1993—back in the day when tarragon and raspberry vinegars first hit supermarket shelves. Nineteen ninety-three was the year in which advanced market research concluded that Milwaukee shoppers preferred their poultry trimmed, deboned, and ready to fry. Whitney introduced its first chocolate yogurt in 1993, and at the annual food-service conference held in Dallas, food marketing gurus advised deli retail executives to sell the sizzle. Cheese sales were on the rise in 1993, and Oscar Mayer

Foods came out with a new line of seasoned hot dogs called Oscar Mayer Big and Juicy. *Supermarket News* noted that the new dogs had been created "with adult tastes in mind." It was right about this time that the term *gastroporn* began to gain widespread acceptance in the English language.

In 1993 the Food Network made its debut on cable television.

The brain-in-the-gut theory can go far to explain the profound satisfactions of 900-pound cheeses, 600-pound supergrills, 240-foot ovens, and the general prevalence of American food mania. And the more I watched the Food Network, the more I began to believe its celebrations represented a climax of sorts in the history of the American stomach. Here twitched the ultimate forms of our digestive monomania: On television the closer the shot, the more detail revealed, the more fetishized the food—the more satisfaction for the enteric brain and the greater the viewership. What could compare?

Only one thing: pornography. An obvious example of the attractions of the involuntary, porn has become a $10 billion industry, roughly equivalent to the GNP of Bolivia. Content providers like Wicked Pictures, Sin City, Adam & Eve, and Vivid Entertainment have proved irresistible to distributors like Rupert Murdoch's News Corporation, Time Warner, AT&T, Marriott, and Hilton International. Prior to selling its interest to Murdoch's News Corporation, General Motors disseminated more sex films than Larry Flynt. Twenty-one million Americans visit the Internet's sixty thousand smut sites each month, and the porn video-rental market accounts for about 700 million rentals a year. In fact, it is the expanding dominion of the gut brain that has propelled pornography from the social ghetto to social diffusion and Jenna Jameson from the back pages of *Nugget* to the center of *US Magazine*, just as it has driven cooking shows from the commercial backwaters of public television to the big time.

When it comes to video and television, the brain-in-the-gut theory becomes practice: Whether on the Food Network or the Hot Network, ESPN, ABC, or CBS, gut reaction hauls in the ratings. As Van Gordon Sauter preached in the 1980s, even hard news needs the emo, and all media executives now understand that the emo comes from the gut. The gut makes the wow, and the wow makes the money. It's not the content that matters—food, murder, or sex—so much as the autonomic form.

Gut reaction drives the ratings, it drives our politics, and it even drives that most sacrosanct of all American contemplations, the business decision. "Even when we're doing food television, it still has to be great television," explained Bob Tuschman, the Food Network's senior vice president for programming and production. "And it is dependent on having great stars, the person who walks into the room and you cannot take your eyes off them. You are enthralled. When I met Rachael Ray, I had the same feeling. When I met Giada De Laurentiis, I felt the same thing. The star quality."

Tuschman paused. He searched for some expression that might communicate what it was the food-show host or hostess possessed that the rest of us did not. Then he smiled. He had found the right word. "Wow," he said.

Before he began his career in television, Bob Tuschman studied political science at Princeton, where he imbibed the transnational spirit of Woodrow Wilson. "You think I'm a Food Network zealot," he declared. "I think we do a great service to the world. We have tapped into a cultural need and desire and want. We are going to continue what we're doing. I think we're on the path."

So far as I knew, no one had ever explored the media's relationship to America's brain in the gut, particularly when it came to gastroporn. But in order to understand why cooking on television reaches more than 90 million households, in order to understand why its share of the market has been growing more than twice as fast as MTV's, and almost triple CNN's rate, I needed to find a new kind of expert, someone who understood the theory of involuntary response, someone who was adept in the technical details of pornography, and someone who watched food television. I found all three in Barbara Nitke.

Nitke began her career as a porn still-photographer in 1982 on the set of *The Devil in Miss Jones, Part II*, which took ten days to film, had a crew of twenty-five, and a budget of $100,000. That was the longest shoot she ever worked on. (These days, a typical porn director may create six feature-length movies in one straight twenty-hour video-sex marathon, for a total cost of $10,000.) Since *Devil*, Nitke has worked on the sets of more than three hundred porn films, which she said is not a huge number, considering that ten thousand new releases enter the market each year. Her most recent gig was with famed feminist porn director Candida Royalle.

I had come to Nitke's studio apartment on the eastern shore of midtown Manhattan, near the United Nations, to watch cooking shows with her, and to compare the histories of sex porn and gastro-porn. For the past several weeks, Nitke had been running porn films side by side with Food Network shows, studying the parallels. She had also been analyzing the in-house ads, like a recent one for the network's "Chocolate Obsession Weekend," which promised to "tantalize your taste buds." In this spot a gorgeous model pushed a chocolate strawberry past parted lips as she luxuriated in a bubble bath. The suds shot dissolved into Food Network super-star Emeril Lagasse, who shook his "Essence"—a trademarked blend of salt, paprika, black pepper, granulated garlic, and onion powder—into a pan of frothing pink goo. The camera moved into the frying pan and stayed there. "There's something very visceral about watching the food," said Nitke. "It's very tissue-y. It's hard not to think of flesh when you're looking at these close-ups."

Like sex porn, gastroporn addresses the most basic human needs and functions, idealizing and degrading them at the same time. "You watch porn saying, 'Yes, I could do that,'" explained Nitke. "You dream that you're there, but you know you couldn't. The guy you're watching on the screen, his sex life is effortless. He didn't have to negotiate, entertain her, take her out to dinner. He walked in with the pizza. She was waiting and eager and hot for him."

Which reminded me of my conversation with Food Network Programming VP Bob Tuschman. "We create this sensual, lush world, begging you to be drawn into it," Tuschman had said. "It's a beautifully idealized world. Who wouldn't want to be a part of that world?"

Of course, recipes made onscreen rarely match their printed correlatives in books, or as they appear as text on the Food Network's much visited Web site, foodtv.com. "That's exactly the way the porn thing works," continued Nitke. "The sex, of course, is impossible to replicate. No one gets a blow job like that."

Nitke clicked on her tiny television and we settled into a show called *Food 911*, in which a handsome, sensitive hunk named Tyler Florence travels the nation, kitchen by kitchen, on a quest to liberate home cooks from their culinary frustrations. We watched as a desperate housewife stared at sturdy young Tyler. Could his arroz con pollo quench her flaming desire?

The camera zeroed in as Tyler expertly spread raw chicken breast across a cutting board. "That is the quintessential pussy shot," Nitke said. "The color of it, the texture of it, the camera lingering lovingly over it." Next, Tyler rolled the glistening lips of chicken breast, which miraculously transformed into a thick phallus, which he doused with raw egg. ("The transgendered chicken moment," noted Nitke.)

"I feel a lot of love right now," Tyler told his transfixed acolyte. "This is a sexy dish." Perspiration had begun to bead on the poor woman's forehead, her dark curls had wilted, her lower lip trembled, and as she gasped, the camera caught her low-cut yellow sundress squeezing her breasts. "This is the pizza man," declared Nitke. "There's the helpless woman who can't do it for herself. In walks the cute young guy who rescues her."

The result was inexorable. Eventually Tyler and the housewife would go cheek to cheek, lean forward, open their mouths, taste the chicken and rice, and melt into a flushed-face, simultaneous food swoon. When this inevitable sequence finally rolled, the editor kept looping their wet mouths and rapt faces as they pushed forkful after forkful of arroz con pollo past their lips, chewed, and swallowed— and pushed and chewed and swallowed again and again. "Classic porn style," said Nitke.

Next up was the great Emeril Lagasse, who has single-handedly replaced the stay-at-home mom's afternoon soap opera, and perhaps her four o'clock fuck. Hunched, lumpen, with a clearly evident bald spot, he possesses the boozy charisma of an über-prole, and his "Bam!" and "Let's kick it up a notch" have become verbal icons of the medium. Fourteen cookbooks bear the name Emeril. His Essences and Rubs are now available in eleven varieties. More than 150 food and kitchen products flash the Lagasse trademark, including three lines of pots and pans, nonstick and stainless Emerilware, Emerilware utensils, Emeril cutlery, an Emeril blender, and an Emeril smoker. Not to mention the Emeril barbecue and pasta sauces, bastings and marinades, salsas and mustards.

Today Emeril Lagasse was making po'boy sandwiches. It was a rerun, but as in traditional porn, so in classic daytime gastroporn—reruns don't matter, and neither do beginnings, middles, or ends. "The big thing in porn is you can't have too much story line," explained Nitke. "It detracts from the sex. Same thing here. Nothing detracts from those food shots."

Emeril jabbed his fists, grunted, then made a guttural promise to demonstrate "that food of love thing. See dat?" he asked, holding up a dripping crawfish. "Just place it in there like such. I think you get the drift." He leaned into the camera, his face framed above the gurgling saucepan. "Look at this. Unbelievable! Oh yeah, babe." The phrase reminded Barbara Nitke of a retired porn actor named George Payne, who had a habit of repeating the exact same expression. "George was famous for his ad-libbing," recalled Nitke. "'Little girl likes that, yeah, babe?' I can hear Emeril saying, 'Little girl likes that—yeah, babe?'"

Next it was time for Rachael Ray, who has shows in both daytime and prime-time Food Network slots, a multimillion dollar book deal, the covers of *People* magazine and the *National Enquirer*, and a paradigm evident to all. "She's the girl next door," cooking-show hostess Sara Moulton explained to me. "She's the girl next door," Bob Tuschman had said.

Near the beginning of her amazing career, Ms. Ray pleasantly surprised her aficionados with a series of images published by the laddie magazine *FHM.* Subsequently disseminated over the Internet, the most popular of these photographs proved to be one of "Ray-Ray" (as her fans call her) in frilly underwear, licking chocolate syrup from the tip of a pendulous wooden spoon. In another shot Ray sat with her legs kicked up on a kitchen counter, her bare thighs smeared with egg whites.

Now Barbara Nitke and I watched Ray-Ray do her perky act with a ripe tomato. "I love just giving it a good smash with the palm of my hand," she bubbled. "A good whack. Then I run my knife through it." Her glistening fingers closed around the dripping fruit.

Noted Nitke, "She gets her hands dirty. It's next-door-neighbor sex, in a kitchen where you've just fucked all over the stove."

Of course, the girl next door is not the only female porn archetype. For every Mary Ann there's a Ginger, and the Food Network's resident glamazon would be Giada De Laurentiis. Giada, Bob Tuschman explained, "has a huge following. She has filled out her skin and really fills out the TV screen." Sara Moulton put it more reductively: "She's eye candy."

Nitke and I watched as Giada prepared some Italian cookies. As usual she was dressed in a tight, sleeveless top. "Now I can touch the dough and elongate it," she said. "I'm getting it all over my fingers." When Giada squeezed a lemon, the camera moved in for a close-up of the abundant yellow stream. "All that juice," came Giada's thick voice-over. "Oh my god," said Nitke. "It's watersports."

Giada promised that her panna cotta would be smooth and creamy in your mouth, then she poured the honey: "Look how easily the honey comes out. Wow . . ."

The camera lingered on Giada's face, then on her hands as she began to chop the garlic—quickly, hypnotically. "That's the equivalent of the sexual skills," Nitke said. "The chopping—that's the hanging-from-the-chandelier-having-sex moment."

When it came time for *Iron Chef*, the simmering black cauldrons reminded Nitke of films such as *Leather-Bound Dykes from Hell* and *Dresden Diaries*. Amid the shooting flames, billowing smoke, and exotic insignia of Kitchen Stadium stood the hyperserious host in his ruffled brocade cape and black leather glove. Imperial music blared as a great tray of writhing squid slowly dropped from the ceiling.

"The black walls, spotty lighting, and low camera angles suggest that the *Iron Chef* guys are the domly doms," said Nitke. The domly doms? Nitke explained her reference to the dominators of sadomasochistic fetish porn. "They're offered these submissive squid, then subject the squid to becoming their creation." As a slave descends into the S&M dungeon to undergo strange transformations, so the squid, through extreme mediation, would eventually find itself squid risotto.

"I will add butter and shortening," said Sara Moulton, who had hosted dump-and-stir television shows for nine years and taped more than a thousand segments. Finally in the studio, I watched the author of *Sara's Secrets for Weeknight Meals* and *Sara Moulton Cooks at Home* as she stood in the middle of her mise-en-scène, a setup very much like the classic stove and counter of her mentor, Julia Child. "I will give a few pulses of the food processor," Moulton continued, "add cheese, give four more pulses."

More than a dozen people huddled around the star. There were the executive, assistant, associate, and culinary producers, the director and the technical director, and the camera operators, production assistants, and food stylists. When the group broke, stylists buffed plush white buns and molded mustard while someone from makeup touched up the star's face and repainted her lips. Moulton's hair, which hung straight and blond, had been sprayed into compliance. Behind Moulton, kitchen windows opened to a faux outdoors, and a side door had been left ajar to reveal the overburdened shelves of a glowing pantry. No matter how cloudy it became in Manhattan, Moulton's kitchen remained sunny; no matter how much she cooked, her pantry stayed full. And I remembered William Alcott's complaint from 1846:

> A modern epicure is almost always eating
> the present dish as a kind of introduction to
> something else.

Moulton rehearsed her Kabuki while Food Network staff in Food Network shirts stenciled with the Food Network's orange logo scrubbed peelers and whisks, stainless spatulas and serrated knives. And as soon as all was dry and in the proper place, yet another intern wheeled out a fresh harvest from the test kitchens.

Within this realm, hunger remains a constant—
or of absolutely no consequence whatsoever. Of
course, the great gastrosophists of the nineteenth
century had long sought to transcend the mundane
limitations of appetite. As the Beecher sisters
solemnly asserted,

It is possible to put much more into the
stomach than can be digested. To guide and
regulate in this matter, the sensation called
hunger is provided.

Ah, yes. Hunger. But even as the interns and
crew aligned the grated cheese and ground chuck
downstairs, Sara Moulton and her director Jeff Kay
(not to mention the executive, assistant, associate,
and culinary producers), knew Bob Tuschman was
upstairs, monitoring ratings, watching videos of new
talent, and obsessing over the recondite desires of
that key demographic, the eighteen- to thirty-five-
year-old male, can't-cook-won't-cook crowd—the
men who like to watch. Turns out that as people
ogle cooking shows more and more, they cook less
and less. "What was educational became a comfort
network," Jeff Kay said to me later. "Watching food
TV is like taking an Ativan."

"Stand by," announced Jen, the production assistant in charge of minutes and seconds. The
Steadicam approached Moulton, who was sipping
herbal tea through a straw, so as not to smudge her
lipstick. "Thirty seconds!" called Jen, who glared at

an overdiligent food-stylist intern who was still pomading the mustard.

"Clear the set!"

"Okay," Jeff Kay's amplified voice boomed from the control room through the public-address system. "Here we go, folks. Tight shot. Rolling tape." Outside the studio, it had finally begun to snow; but here, where weeks of episodes compact into days, the twelve banks of kliegs blasted the warmth of an eternal spring.

"Go ahead," the Steadicam operator murmured to Moulton. "Cook."

"Ten seconds . . ."

Kay's voice engulfed the soundstage. "Quiet on the set!"

Theme music welled up, the monitors flashed to life, and everything else receded into darkness and silence, all except the flat, sweet, Midwestern accent of a solitary voice.

"Hi. I'm Sara Moulton, executive chef of *Gourmet* magazine. Today we'll explore the great American hamburger . . ."

Two takes and a half hour later, the time came for Sara Moulton and her special guest, southern food scholar John T. Edge, to cook onion burgers and make apple pie. The difficulty would be doing it together, on camera. But there was one thing everybody in the studio understood: At the very end of the episode, Moulton would hold steady the uncovered pie, and Edge would smash the crust on top.

Jeff Kay sat in the control room, which bore more than a passing resemblance to the bridge of the *Starship Enterprise*. Kay was delivering orders into his headset. "Go three," he said. "Music up. Dissolve two. And dissolve. Take two. Dissolve four."

Moulton sliced onions while Edge grabbed handfuls of ground chuck. "It's kind of a free-form hamburger," Edge told a pedestal camera.

Charged with the energy of live television, each shot delivered an autonomic tingle. *Taste life,* I remembered. . . . And now all the cams closed in as Edge slapped handfuls of ground beef into a smoking pan, then turned his attention to the apple pie.

"Music up," said Kay. "Dissolve two. And dissolve. Lose the matte. Two to three . . ."

Moulton dropped apples into the food processor and pulsed four times. Edge moved in and poured a powdery stream of cayenne pepper. "That's not a full teaspoon," whispered an assistant producer.

On the floor the ONE MINUTE sign went up. Edge scooped the dripping, peppered apples and tumbled the chunks into a pie dish. Jeff Kay dissolved to a close-up of the dough, which Sara Moulton unceremoniously whacked a couple of times with an oversize rolling pin. Edge grabbed the unfinished apple pie and brought it over to Moulton, who held it in front of her belly.

She did not look entirely comfortable in the pose, nor as certain of herself as when she was peeling and coring those apples—as though she were as perplexed by the act she found herself committing as she was dumbfounded by the future of food media itself. ("I have no idea what it's gonna be," she ruefully admitted to me later. "None, zero, zip, zilch. You never know; it's so changed.")

Thirty seconds . . .

As the jib shot of spice-slathered apples filled the monitors, I remembered the words of the great Puritan divine Cotton Mather:

> Roasted apples with milk may now and then
> be allow'd of . . .

But the reverend never could have envisioned this conglomeration of fruit, cheese, and spice, much less the strange choreography: John T. Edge grasped the perfectly rolled circle of glistening dough, which hung low and loose in fleshy sags; then in a quick, overhand thrust, he slammed it on top of Moulton's fruit. In extreme close-up, the dough quivered, then lay still.

Cameras stopped and culinary assistants swarmed, shoving what had become a rather bedraggled and sorry looking apple pie off to the side, next to a lukewarm onion burger. The pie of the money shot would not be the pie Moulton and Edge had climactically smashed together. It was a "swap" pie, crafted in Food Network test kitchens, and it was absolutely gorgeous. But its momentary perfection was sobering, too. Fruit ripens to die, Nielsens rise to fall. Sara Moulton would tell me later that after more than a thousand shows, her contract with the Food Network was not to be renewed. ("Listen, I'm not stupid," she would say. "Every show has a life. Every personality has a life.")

Then the lights went down and without negotiation or hint of pretense, Sara Moulton and John T. Edge went at it. Moulton's food swoon was well practiced, a controlled, quiet rapture, while Edge's bliss was more jubilant and rakish, as though each bite was another hit in a lifelong succession of thrills. They ate standing up, straight from the serving dish. They ate without speaking, without napkins, without stopping. When they gobbled the apple pie, it was as if the serpent had never slithered down that ancient tree.

The Sweet Taste of God

No remedy is to be compared unto a vomit. It will do, when all other methods and medicines fail.

—Cotton Mather, 1724

By being acquainted with the sympathy between the head and stomach we may remove puking by bleeding, and a headache by puking.

—Benjamin Rush, 1812

Washington Irving may have been the first to articulate America's food mania; the Food Network may have been the first to perfect autonomic media; but the Pilgrims had been the first to arrive hungry. And despite their cliché reputation as stern antisensualists, the Puritan settlers revered the grand central eminence of the stomach; and the gut returned the favor and became a wellspring of their power. Odd as it may sound, the origins of our food mania—the fetishes, the obsessions, the passions, and the gastroporn—date back to these first digesters of the New World.

The generally accepted starting point for a history of the American stomach can be found in the sixth chapter of *Mourt's Relation*, in a letter written by Edward Winslow dated December 12, 1621:

> Our harvest being gotten in, our Governor sent four men on fowling, that so we might after a more special manner rejoice together, after we had gathered the fruit of our labors; they four in one day killed as much fowl, as with a little help beside, served the company almost a week, at which time amongst other recreations, we exercised our arms, many of the indians coming amongst us, and amongst the rest their greatest King Massasoyt, with some ninety men, whom for three days we entertained and feasted, and they went out and killed five deer, which they brought to the plantation and bestowed on our Governor, and upon the Captain, and others. And although it be not always so plentiful as it was at this time with us, yet by the goodness of God we are so far from want that we often wish you partakers of our plenty.

Here were the Pilgrims and the Wampanoags and Squanto and Standish frolicking amid the pleasant, iconic anecdote: the first Thanksgiving.

No bill of fare remains extant, but the experts have estimated it was a party for 140. They generally agree it featured roast duck, roast goose, roast partridge, roast venison, roast oysters, and baked Indian (which was what the colonists called corn). But the Pilgrims did not repeat their celebration on the same day the following year, nor any year thereafter in commemoration—for these men and women did not feast according to the calendar but according to the spirit.

The Puritans modeled themselves after the ancient Israelites, who had been blessed with manna from the sky every day they wandered through the wilderness, not to mention the big meals on Passover, Pentecost, and Purim. Father Abraham himself had hosted numerous mighty barbecues, as had Isaac, Samson, Solomon, Levi, and Lot. So when John Winthrop's wife and family arrived at the new Jerusalem, they were greeted by a majestic parade, ceremonial volleys of shot, and staggering loads of butchered kids, venison, poultry, geese, partridges, and not particularly kosher hogs. In fact, whenever ships from Europe arrived, great banquets would follow. Whenever the boats brought good tidings or when hostile plans against the settlers had been foiled, thanksgiving feasts would be proclaimed. Whenever the Pequots lost a battle, the Puritans partook. Whenever the settlers signed treaties with the Mohegans or the Narragansetts, they ate.

The Puritans had abandoned the European continent precisely because they despised the rituals of the Catholics and the Church of England, among them the rigid succession of Friday feasts that honored whoever happened to be saint of the week. The great precedent for refusing to participate in the customary—and thus depraved—religious banqueting of the Old World had been articulated almost half a century before the first Thanksgiving in the New World. In a *Confession of Faith*, written from Newgate prison in 1572, religious nonconformists John Field and Thomas Wilcocks declared an act of digestive disobedience:

> We think that those feast-days of Christ, as of his birth, circumcision, passover, resurrection and ascension, etc., may, by Christian liberty be kept, because they are only devoted to Christ, to whom all days and times belong. But days dedicated to saints, with fasts on their eves, we utterly dislike . . .

The new nonschedule of feasting and fasting not only became fundamental to the Puritans' antiestablishment religious observance, but to their understanding of moral history. When to eat and when not to eat became a foundation for their relationship with God. Furthermore, the Puritans believed that the relative strength or weakness of a person's divine connection could be discerned through the relative health or sickness of the body. "Let thy bad stomach put thee in mind of thy neglecting to digest that Word," chided Mather, "that should be more to thee, than thy necessary food."

Even before they left the European continent, the Puritans had gathered in secret to fast and to feast as the spirit demanded. Not only did they fast for divine guidance before they even considered the question of coming to America, not only did they fast before making the final decision to come here, but as the departure date neared, they fasted again. On the day of their embarkation, the Puritans fasted. As their boats lost sight of England and passed into the vast desert of the Atlantic, they fasted again. Safely landed on the shores of America, the Puritans got down on their knees and thanked God. Then they fasted.

Francis Higginson and company reached Salem in 1629; John Winthrop arrived in Boston in 1630. On Wednesdays and Thursdays of the voyage, both companies fasted. This was most certainly not the way things had been done in merry old England, where Friday had meant abstinence followed by a feast. But it does explain why we celebrate Thanksgiving on Thursday.

Pilgrim PR had advertised the journey into the wilderness as a value-added venture: spiritual nirvana that also provided fresh running water, plenty of firewood, and easy access to leeks and onions. But that was not what the settlers found.

> A grievous sickness, induced largely by the hardships of the voyage, was upon them . . .

Thus wrote William DeLoss Love, the greatest (and perhaps the only) nineteenth-century scholar of Puritan ingestion. Professor Love devoted his academic career to early American feast and fast days, and his life's work consisted of a 514-page doorstop study of Puritan eating and noneating that, sadly, has not seen print since 1895.

"Many died," continued Love:

> It seemed best to the main body of the colonists, then located at Charlestown, to keep a day of humiliation "to pacify the Lord's wrath."

The day of humiliation was Love's code for a day of fasting. And on July 30, 1630, all the settlers in all the settlements bonded in hunger. This first united fast of America was so widely and enthusiastically observed that in the ensuing years the authorities wielded much civil control through repeated digestive interventions. In the eight decades between 1620 and 1700, the Puritan theocracy would ordain 664 days of regulated eating (approximately one for every two months, eighty years running), and the majority of them were not feasts but fasts.

One year, when Roxbury and Boston both wanted to hire the same ministers, congregation leaders instituted rival fasts to judge the most worthy settlement. Meetings of New England's ruling elite often devolved into disputes about whether circumstances merited full or empty bellies, as in this 1690 entry from Samuel Sewall's diary:

> Mr. Torrey is for a fast or at least a fast first. Mr. Willard for a Thanksgiving first. Mr. Torrey fears lest a Thanksgiving should tend to harden people in their carnal confidence. . . .

And so on. Thus did binge-eating spiked with self-induced starvation find its earliest footholds. Like Pallas Athena, bulimarexia emerged fully formed from the New England mind.

When Anne Hutchinson dared interpret the word of God in her own house, without the permission of higher authorities, they banished her from the Massachusetts Bay Colony into the howling wilderness (i.e., Rhode Island). As a matter of course, the crisis demanded its own public fast day, "for humiliation and prayer." John Winthrop declared that if anybody in his colony refused to stop eating, they, too, would be "guilty of sedition, and also of contempt."

Indeed, the Puritans fasted against all visible and invisible signs of disrespect directed against their rule, just as they fasted against oppression, atheism, superfluity, idleness, and perilous novelties. They fasted through periods of political agitation just as they fasted after earthquakes, thunder, hailstones, hurricanes, fires, floods, and droughts. They fasted to abolish profanity, drunkenness, unrighteousness, smallpox, high fevers, and sleeping during sermons. They fasted when the weather turned frigid, when the snow heaped down upon their heads, and when the wind blew colder than anyone had ever imagined it could blow. They fasted to fight cankerworms, palmerworms, and ungodly swarms of grasshoppers and insects. When prices for Indian corn and rye meal spiraled out of control, the government ordered "a Day of Public Fasting & Prayer" to atone for "their many heinous and provoking Sins." In 1663 they fasted against the mildew on the wheat.

Every late spring ushered in the starving time, a six-week gap after supplies from the previous autumn had been consumed but before the new crops could be harvested, a time, wrote John Winthrop, Jr., "of extreme Scarcitie" and "terrible Famine." It was then the Puritans fasted against hunger.

As early as the spring of 1642, John Winthrop had decreed a fast to purify England and Ireland. Only twenty-two years after Plymouth Rock and the Puritan stomach had already begun to meddle in foreign affairs. From then on, whenever the bishops in Germany adopted popish doctrines, the Chosen in America would not touch their food. And the purview of the American gut extended to outer space. A comet appeared in the winter of 1664–65, zodiacal light "which seemed to have an ominous semblance to a spear pointed toward new England." Faced with such a symbol of doom, the Puritans fasted—and the comet disappeared. Yes, New England may have been a cold and dark expanse, rife with disease and danger beyond anyone's control, but the settlers could command their stomach, the center of their quivering nervous system. So they bargained and cajoled Yahweh the only way they could.

In June of 1692 witches swooped down upon Salem, Massachusetts, and possessed a nine-year-old named Betty Parris. Betty was the daughter of Samuel Parris, the town's minister. Parris and his wife had come to Salem from Barbados accompanied by an Arawak slave named Tituba, who became the first suspected witch. Of course, Minister Parris ordered his household to fast. Sarah Osborne, an old woman who had not attended church for more than a year, and whom Parris also suspected of witchcraft, was ordered to fast with them.

Soon the neighboring ministers had begun to fast in sympathy. More private fasts followed, and all these excesses of noneating worked as an accelerant for the growing nervous excitement, the whispered demands that Osborne and Tituba should die. Then Minister Parris ordered the entire village of Salem off food, to seek the Lord that he would rebuke Satan and be a light unto his people in this day of darkness.

The Puritans' most sensitive instrument—the stomach—had fairly proven demonic presence, so after the fasting was finished, the next proposed solution to the problem was food. Diabolical food. At the urging of a neighbor, Tituba and her husband mixed rye meal with the urine of one of the possessed children and whipped up a witch cake. Such a delicacy, if fed to one of the devil's consorts (a warlock, perhaps, or the local Obi doctor), was supposed to reveal the identities of those responsible for the satanic afflictions. As per instructions, Tituba fed her witch cake to Minister Parris's dog, but no extant records describe whether or not the canine would confess. Either way, the Antichrist was not appeased.

So the authorities hauled Tituba Indian and Sarah Osborne (and a local vagrant named Sarah Good) off to jail—where Osborne promptly died— and the Salem witch trials were soon featuring testimony about "days of hellish feasts and thanksgivings" diabolically ordained by the defendants. Some witnesses went so far as to testify that when Tituba and Sarah Osborne had come near their house, their cheese had soured and their butter turned bad. What more damning evidence could there be?

One year and twenty executions later, it occurred to the authorities that the urine-cake, abominable-feast, and butter-gone-bad case for the prosecution might not have been as compelling as once seemed. Now convinced of the error of their ways, the Puritans racked their brains for some way to repent for their sins.

They decided to fast.

Washington Irving asserted in his *History of New York* that the earliest leadership of this Dutch "colony of huge feeders" consisted of burgomasters who were "generally chosen by weight." The chiefs were

> the best fed men in the community; feasting lustily on the fat things of the land, and gorging so heartily on oysters and turtles, that in process of time they acquire the activity of the one, the form, the waddle, and the green fat of the other.

The first families of Manhattan Island were, in fact, defined by what they consumed: The Van Courtlands were "great killers of wild ducks"; the Van Winkles, "potent suckers of eggs." Thus, according to Irving, New York was in its early Dutch days nearly a perfect place, for

> it is an incontrovertible fact, well known to your skillful physiologists, that the high road to the affections is through the throat.

A few hundred miles to the north, the Puritans had reached similar conclusions about the vital link between eating and emotion. What was melancholia but an ulcer of the mind? "He that would have a Clear Head," wrote Cotton Mather, "must have a Clean Stomach." And in the centuries following Mather, the New England digestive tract assumed a position of paramount importance in science, medicine, and protopsychology. Digestive diseases were soon classified as nervous diseases, just as anorexia and bulimia are now understood to be psychological disorders, just as people undergo psychological counseling to cure obesity, just as eating too much junk food was declared by legal scholars in the late 1970s to be a valid indicator of insanity.

By the time the American Revolution loomed, our bellies and our psyches were ready. In 1765, the year of the Stamp Act, the colony of Connecticut declared a fast day to preserve its "most dear and valuable rights and privileges." New Hampshire and Massachusetts soon followed suit, and in the nine years from 1774 to 1783, every feast and fast day ordained within the American colonies—147 in all—was somehow, someway, in reference to the war against the British. In both 1775 and 1776 Massachusetts, New Hampshire, and Connecticut each proclaimed three separate and distinct fast days, and Rhode Island fasted twice. In both years absolutely everyone stopped eating for one additional day in a monumental show of sacrifice for the "United

Colonies." Declared by the Continental Congress, July 20, 1775, became our first official national fast day. One year later, as the Declaration of Independence was being signed, Massachusetts lawmakers were busy issuing their own much less famous proclamation—announcing a statewide fast.

Perhaps as a result of the great success fasting had enjoyed during the Revolution, refusing food became mandatory as future wars were contemplated. In 1798 President Adams declared a national day of "solemn humiliation, fasting, and prayer" to palliate the terrors of citizens on the eve of what many supposed would be inevitable hostilities with France. As the War of 1812 loomed, President Madison appointed a national fast day so that each and every citizen could implore God to nourish American public counsels, feed our patriotism, and stoke the caissons and six-inch brass howitzers.

American public fasting remained a respected political strategy well into the nineteenth century. In 1841 a national fast honored the memory of President Harrison. In 1849 President Taylor ordered a fast "on account of the cholera." On June 1, 1865, the country mourned Lincoln with a fast. It was not until 1894, after two hundred annual exercises of state-mandated noneating, that the Commonwealth of Massachusetts finally abolished its spring fast day.

Just as fasting had endured as a public and political matter, so it endured as a medical concern. Only noneating sanctioned by the proper authorities could be salubrious. Practiced any other way, it was sick. As far back as the days of the Pilgrims, a pernicious and prolonged refusal to eat had already been well established as a bona fide disease: "a grievous decay and failure of Appetite." Cotton Mather, who had been a close observer of hysterical pre-teen Puritans, may have recalled certain symptoms of demonic possession when he wrote his voluminous medical treatise, *The Angel of Bethesda*, and may have been the first American settler to describe what has since become a very familiar syndrome:

> A considerable quantity of a flegmatic humour or, of a bilious humour gathered in the stomach, may be sufficient alone to produce this inappetency. There may also be other causes for it. . . .

We see here the clinical ancestor of the much-dreaded, much-sensationalized antidigestive psychological plague of our own age, anorexia nervosa. We may feel superior to Mather's primitive descriptions of phlegmatic humours and angered constitutions, but the quest for the cure remains current.

According to statistics published by the National Eating Disorders Association, of those diagnosed with long-term anorexia 5 to 20 percent will ultimately die as a direct result. Not only does anorexia have the highest mortality rate of any mental illness, it has spawned a glut of research, hundreds of clinics, demi-empires of publishing, and more Google hits than the war in Iraq. Today you can treat your fasting disorder through biobehavioral phenotyping, PET imaging, proton-pump inhibitors, or Christ—which was roughly the same range of treatments available in the seventeenth century, give or take a few MRIs. If Cotton Mather's abstruse yet "most efficacious" cure for the disease (a volatile mixture of chalk, wormwood, oil of mint, and syrup of quinces) could not resuscitate a gastric system ruined by prolonged fasting, he offered as antidote the following prayer: "Let an Appetite for an Appetite, be now raised in thy Soul."

Yet the American disease had also been an American cure. Having been granted widespread political and religious legitimacy from the earliest days, the Puritan fast had long presented itself as a remedy, kind of like the herbal, cleansing juice fast that has become ensconced in the realm of alternative therapy today. Not eating was an essential element of Cotton Mather's prescription for jaundice:

> The urine of an healthy lad, six ounces, with six drams of white sugar; drunk fasting . . .

Here, the fast led to health as efficiently as any diet guru's regimen. Just like that therapeutic urine.

"One's own urine," added Mather,

mixed with the yolk of an egg, and sweet-
ened with a little sugar, taken for a while, has
cured the coughs and other ails, of those that
have been thought far gone in consumption.

My history of the American stomach was never
meant to include such culinary practices, but now it
was too late. Mather was already suggesting the ingestion of "crude urine" as a remedy for worms,
fevers, colds, cavities, earaches, ulcers, bruises, consti-
pation, cancer, and "falling-sickness." And slurping
urine, I suspected, was only the beginning.

Mather cited dozens of scientific authorities before declaring sheep dung a "sovereign remedy"; then
there were the esteemed doctors who promoted pig
dung and rat dung, pigeon dung and hen dung (but
only "the white part," dried and cut with sugar and
white wine). For the colicky baby, Mather and his dis-
tinguished cohorts suggested a few cloves of garlic in-
fused in white wine, "to which add a little juice of
horse-dung; —and say nothing." Even dog excrement
possessed "its virtues." And as for the cure "against
all diseases," the great medical panacea—it was nothing but cow patties dunked in springwater.

Let them stand for digestion twenty-four
hours; and then decant the brown tincture.

Clearly, a history of American anorexia would lead
to a cornucopia of related if equally unsavory top-

ics, such as the history of early American puking, which has never before been attempted. Like it or not, this will be a first. As a courtesy to the reader, I have tried to keep this section short, but I could not skip the subject altogether, essential as it is to the tale.

No remedy could hold a candle to a good vomit—that was the standard Puritan reduction of the issue. If evil was real (which it was), if Satan was corporeal (which he was), then both could exist within our bodies (which they did), which meant they must be expelled (and there were many channels). The Puritans' reliance on emetics of all shapes, sizes, and forms made it possible to vomit up our sin.

The Puritans accepted the fact that in order to live they had to ingest something that was dead. Three times a day death entered their bodies: first through the mouth, then through the intestinal tract, that part of the system most intimate with filth and morbidity. Through the miracle of transubstantiation (i.e., digestion), the stomach could resurrect the spirit of life from the throes of mortality, while the remainder—the dead part of death— could be excreted.

The Puritans, perhaps necessarily, adored laxatives and diuretics. After all, if a chunk of living death happened to get stuck inside your esophagus or colon, the results could be dire. By 1724 Cotton Mather had explored all aspects of the issue. But first, an extremely curtailed biography: The Reverend John Cotton (1584–1652) of the First Church of Boston, and the Reverend Richard Mather

(1596–1669) of the First Church of Dorchester, were Cotton's grandfathers. Dad was the legendary Increase, president of Harvard, author of 175 published works. Young Cotton was born in 1663 and enrolled at Harvard eleven years later. Some scholars tell us he studied medicine, even considered becoming a doctor instead of a minister. All agree that the boy obsessively sought communion with God.

Intent on shattering Increase's records, Cotton would eventually publish 468 staggeringly miscellaneous literary works, from political tracts, fantastic allegories, and hard-nosed foreign-policy statements to lengthy meditations on how to evade demonic possession. For Cotton believed in predestination, eternal damnation, and hybridization in plants. He followed developments in geology, botany, and the conversion of the Jews. Yes, he was superstitious, trembling at the shape of an ominous cabbage. But as Salem had proved, witchcraft was not so much opposed to hard science as a science in and of itself, and Cotton Mather adored science, convinced as he was that the bodies of the natural world reflected both the glory of God and the iniquitous manifestations of the Antichrist. Above all, he believed his soul was, as he liked to put it, the Main Digester.

In fact, Cotton Mather's devotion to Christ Almighty, his devotion to medicine, and his devotion to the stomach could not be separated. His beliefs all came straight from the good book: Jehoram did a bloody thing, Mather wrote in reference to one of the more obscure kings of Israel, who by the age of thirty-two had not only murdered his six brothers but allowed the sin of fornication within the precincts of Jerusalem. Payback time came when Yahweh nailed Jehoram with a particularly nasty digestive ailment: His bowels fell out. To a close reader of the Bible such as Mather, this vengeance revealed the worst of all possible fates, spiritual and physical: the digestive tract, being out of order, how many and how miserable the consequences!

Consider the following seventeenth-century Puritan meditation, as suggested by Mather:

Have I not wanted bowels toward them, whom I should have been compassionately concerned for?

Since the bowel was generally accepted as the medical seat of sympathy and the physical origin of all emotional attachment, Mather's biological prayer served as the equivalent of the Golden Rule. Love your neighbor, love their bowels.

In adolescence Mather discovered that by denying his stomach for extended periods of time, he could hear the angels sing, experience ecstatic visions, and savor (as the great Puritan divine Jonathan Edwards would put it half a century later) the sweet taste of God in his mouth.

He sacrificed hours to silent devotion and hours to spirited musical renditions of the psalms. Sometimes he fasted on his knees, sometimes as he lay prone on the floor. Often, like any perfection-loving, self-hating, modern-day anorectic, he wept. Throughout the sixty-five years of his life, Mather lamented and rejoiced through hundreds of days without food, and his compulsive not-eating resulted in a severe case of something he eventually identified as splenetic maladies, a condition that encompassed a wide variety of gastrointestinal irregularities. Mather's piety may have finally transformed and redeemed the peristalsis of the winding inner serpent, Mather's gut. But it hurt like hell.

In classic Puritan fashion, Mather had been taught that the world was soaked in wickedness. He knew that despite everything he did, he could be heading straight to the inferno. He knew his body was the seat of utter depravity, knew his stomach oozed filth, so he could have easily dismissed human appetite—from the first apple to last night's stewed pumpkin—as nothing but the detritus of our bestial nature and left it at that. But Cotton Mather had also inherited a streak of nonconformity. He publicly advocated smallpox inoculation, which was at the time a controversial, wildly unpopular policy. While many of his peers believed that extermination would be an excellent and judicious solution to their Indian problem, Mather respected and recorded Native American medical remedies. He even allowed his children to sit down to meals beside him at the table, a radical departure from the customary Puritan practice, which demanded that kids stand behind parents, eating what was handed back. As the first bona fide food nut in American history, Mather trumpeted his intimate knowledge of what he called the God of Health. Sure, he was pompous, priggish, and obnoxious. Why should he be any different from all the diet doctors who came after?

The language may be stilted, but the gist of Mather's enteric aphorisms remains current:

> By suppers and surfeits more have been killed than all the physicians in the world have cured.

> Many dishes will breed many diseases.

> Look after thy stomach.

And then he would come up with something truly wacky:

> The conscience is to the SOUL what the stomach is to the body.

To understand what Mather had in mind here may explain much about the American stomach: Puritan doctors assumed that the workings of digestion maintained the most acute intimacy with the rest of the body, a fine-tuned and far-reaching sensibility as delicately calibrated as our spiritual sensitivity to good and evil. For all diseases originated in the stomach, the principal wheel in the animal economy. Jaundice and asthma, consumption and mania—they could all be reduced to digestion.

In his contemplations of the Stomach Depraved, Mather did not flinch from strictly clinical observation:

> Sometimes a violent, yea, a dangerous vomiting, seizes upon people. The enraged bile in their stomach, sets 'em a vomiting, so that if it be not stop'd, their very life is a going. . . .

At the same time, such physical trauma suggested spiritual equivalents:

> . . . Think, O Man: Have I cast up the sins that are poisoning of my soul? The confession of sin is the vomit of the soul. . . . And think: Has not my soul as much amiss in it as my stomach?

An American stomach purged by a vomit typified a Puritan soul redeemed by public confession. Such allegorical affinity meant the Puritans could not simply get stomachaches. Mather's endless lists of gastric maladies—culled from his encyclopedic knowledge of doctors from ancient times to his present—were as varied as the Puritans' endless dockets of sin, ranging from the humoral colic to the flatulent colic, the bilious colic, the convulsive colic, the hysteric colic, the inveterate scorbutic colic, and the dreaded dry bellyache (of this final variety there were several subvarieties, including the rheumatic, the splenetic, and the nervous dry bellyache). Any one of these diseases, improperly treated, could result in death. In all of them, vomits have been known to work wonderful cures.

Not only did Mather cherish his vomits, he adored sudorifics (sweat inducers), sialagogues (saliva inducers), sternutators (sneeze inducers), and venesections (phlebotomy, too, was a matter of relieving occluded flow, a heartburn of the veins). And Mather's passion for cathartics, evacuations, emetics, expectorants, expellers, ebullitions, and diuretics were not unique to him. Like the stomach purge and the artificial vomit, all these techniques to expel morbific matter were generally understood to contribute to the happiness and redemption of both the miserable individual and the suffering world, and became accepted medical practice.

The result of all this stomach theory was simple: Since every aspect of good health could be ascribed to good digestion, almost every remedy for ill health could be reduced to digestion's reverse:

In the case of choking, a vomit may be given very seasonably.

In the case of a cough, a gentle vomit.

In the case of distemper, seasonable vomits.

In the case of asthma, vomit.

In the case of dropsy, a vomit may not be amiss.

In the case of apoplexy, vomits do a deal of good.

In the case of vertigo, vomit.

In the case of jaundice, vomit.

In the case of hiccups, vomit.

In the case of bloody flux, vomit.

In the case of nightmares, vomit.

In the case of shortness of breath, vomiting with warm water three or four times.

In the case of lethargy, vomits and purges and sweats and blisters.

In the case of a coma, more vomits and purges and sweats and blisters.

(After the vomit, perceived Mather, the patient is marvelously relieved.)

Above all other medical techniques, the Puritans sought the vomit that is at our own command. Mather listed the easiest, gentlest, and most fashionable vomits: hot water, warm water, cold water, and olive water; emetic tartar, salt of vitriol, ipecacuanha root (a precursor of today's ipecac), and the syrup of peach blossoms, which may be given to infants, yea, as soon as they are born.

Welcome to the world, kid. Now puke.

Mather knew that at its stewy center the body hosted a visceral struggle for the soul, and what had made him so sure of this fantastic scheme was that he had seen the evidence with his own eyes. The New World's abundance of intestinal parasites personified perverted eating: antistomachs that, by devouring, devoured you. Sin was literally a worm that ate you from the inside out. Mather had witnessed the awful extraction of such villains from a victim's bowel, up through the victim's mouth—and he had trembled at their formidable dimensions:

> I have seen one in my neighbourhood, the head whereof being seized in the throat of the patient by his hand was pull'd up until he was found about one hundred and fifty foot long.

Here, at last, was the vomit that had, in its logical extension, become an exorcism.

We would like to believe that Cotton Mather's obsessions were limited to his own twisted mind, that his lists of drugs and methods of treatments were nothing but superstition spiked with fanaticism. But faith in the catechism of the vomit remained standard American medical theory not only throughout Mather's century, but for centuries to come. Take, for example, the case of Benjamin Rush, the most famous doctor in Revolutionary America, known today as the father of American psychiatry. (The restraining device he designed in 1810—a cross between a side chair and a straitjacket—remains in use throughout modern mental institutions, police interrogation rooms, and torture chambers world round.) Above all other topics in human physiology, Dr. Rush was interested in the human mind. But Rush's idea of the mind might not coincide with our idea of the mind. The mind he was talking about could be "felt in the pulse, in the stomach, and in the liver."

Trained by the greatest doctors of Europe at the world-renowned medical school at the University of Edinburgh, Rush returned to Philadelphia in 1769 to become the most respected and influential medical practitioner in America. He was also a heavy hitter in radical politics, an early backer of Thomas Paine, and a signer of the Declaration of Independence. When the war arrived, George Washington appointed him surgeon general of the Middle Department of the Continental army. And Dr. Rush returned the favor—in a manner of speaking: On a snowy December afternoon in 1799 George Washington complained of a sore throat. His personal physicians convened, and following the renowned theories and practices of the great Dr. Rush, extracted more than two and a half quarts of blood from our first President. He died later that evening.

In the great emetic medical tradition of the Enlightenment, Benjamin Rush knew that the stomach sat in the center of the nervous system, from which position it "sympathized" with the rest of the body, a fact that proved to be extremely practical:

> ... thus by being acquainted with the sympathy between the head and stomach we may

remove puking by bleeding, and a headache by puking . . . By knowing the sympathy between the stomach and feet, we are enabled to translate gout from the stomach to the feet . . . by knowing the sympathy between the liver and stomach, we are enabled to cure dyspepsia by removing hepatitis.

And so on. Thus, every detail of the stomach's intake and discharge had to be monitored and controlled. So Dr. Rush prescribed vast loads of emetics to his patients—along with a baroque variety of errhines and emmenagogues, clysters and cataplasms. The entire body—from the sweat glands to the tongue to the ears—must follow the stomach's example. Rush's infamous bloodletting was but a venous puke.

Rush purged and bled to death almost every patient who crossed his path during Philadelphia's yellow-fever epidemic. But if Rush's methods appear absurd to us, they did not to the majority of America. Before he journeyed across the country, Meriwether Lewis made it a point to stop in Philadelphia for a quick tutoring session with the famed doctor. He knew that the all-meat diet of the explorers would virtually guarantee gastrointestinal maladies. So when he finally set off across the continent, Lewis carried fifty dozen of Dr. Rush's mercury-filled "Bilious Pills," the laxatives his men fondly dubbed thunderclappers.

Unlike Benjamin Rush, whose medical theories and practices have been relegated to the slops of American history, Nathaniel Hawthorne has remained one of the canonical elect, a certified literary genius, clearly not to be considered in the puke chapter of a cranked-up history of the American stomach. But Hawthorne was hardly isolated from the great currents of nineteenth-century American gastrosophy. His sister-in-law, Mary Tyler Peabody Mann (Mrs. Horace Mann), wrote one of the most representative books of Hawthorne's time, *Christianity in the Kitchen*. "Temper, it has been said, lies in the stomach," wrote Mary Mann:

> Every intelligent dyspeptic knows that he is a worse man when suffering under a paroxysm of his malady, than in one of his lucid intervals. ... Why is not dyspepsia disgraceful, like delirium tremens? When it comes to be so considered, as it assuredly will when the gospel of the body is fully understood, it will be banished from good society.

While Hawthorne may have harbored suspicions about the gospel of the body, he was most definitely haunted by the Christian fanaticism of his ancestry. One of his Puritan forebears had sat in judgment at the Salem witch trials. Perhaps we should not be surprised that when Hawthorne came to consider contemporary demonic possession, he focused on the gut.

One of Hawthorne's short stories from 1846 carries the epigastric title: "Egotism; or, The Bosom Serpent." The story's protagonist, Roderick Elliston, is a "lean man, of unwholesome look," his complexion "a greenish tinge over its sickly white." As it turns out, Elliston's problem is more than your garden-variety dyspepsia. He is the "man with a snake in his bosom." And thus Elliston's convulsive alimentary refrain: "It gnaws me! It gnaws me!"

What are we to make of Roderick Elliston's ubiquitous pest, this "odious reptile," this "thing alive"—if not an incarnation of evil, knavery swilling through the intestinal tract, depravity that must come out the way it went in? Near the end of Hawthorne's tale, Elliston stands "before a looking-glass, with his mouth wide open," egotistically mesmerized by his guts. The snake within had digested all unto itself. But just as Elliston checks himself into an asylum for lunatics (a precursor to a present-day high-colonics detox center crossed with a talk-cure ward for anorectics and bulimics), Hawthorne reveals that the demon of the stomach has a peculiar value:

> Whether insane or not, he showed so keen a perception of frailty, error, and vice, that many persons gave him credit for being possessed not merely with a serpent, but with an actual fiend, who imparted this evil faculty of recognizing whatever was ugliest in man's heart.

Roderick Elliston could perceive the serpent lurking within all our guts—perhaps because every one of us suffers from an equivalent perverted obsession with the snake in our own belly. Of course, an actual bosom serpent would go far to explain much American solipsism, why we squander our days and years peering down the collective esophagus.

And why, no matter how much or how little we eat, we never seem to get it right.

The Secret Ingredient

Let us, with our advanced civilization, consecrate our cooking utensils, as the prophet Zachariah predicted they should be consecrated in the "day of the Lord," and regard as sacred those laws of health which, even in the days of Moses, formed the basis of the national code.
— Mary Tyler Peabody Mann, 1857

Eggs and milk are typical or perfect foods.
— Sarah Tyson Rorer, 1902

I told Lizzie that the stomach was the center of the nervous system, the core of all psychology, the master of the mind and sister of the soul; and she told me it was time for a dinner party. Two weeks later she served zucchini puree, Rock Cornish game hens with fresh pasta and string beans, a tossed salad, a cheese course, and a nectarine-and-apricot pie for dessert. During the evening we did not once mention anorexia or vomit, Cotton Mather, Mary Mann,

Benjamin Rush, Nathaniel Hawthorne, or pyloric sphincters. Instead, we talked artisanal.

As it got late the company waxed gastrosophical and we soon transcended the borders of free-range chickens. We reached beyond Julia and Alice and Ayurveda, beyond handpicked and hothouse and heirloom, beyond fusion and frisée. And certainly beyond the paltry boundaries of organic. Organic, as we all knew, had become just another commodity: Whole Foods was nothing more than fifty-nine thousand square feet of supersized capitalism gurgling beneath a flagship Williams-Sonoma.

But the morning after, through a leftover haze of Mouton and Granpomier, it seemed to me as though the insights of our little group had not been illuminated so much as they had been constricted by grass-fed goat, art lettuces, and holistic legumes. I recalled that when dessert had rolled around, a very nice young woman who had grown up on a farm somewhere in the middle prepared to top Lizzie's pie with her house gift, a quart of ice cream. She had made it herself, she told us, from raw milk. Milk straight from the grass-fed cow: unpasteurized, unprocessed, and thus totally forbidden. A reverential silence settled as the contraband vanilla came out of the freezer and I realized this was our pathetic scantling of radical chic, New York City wags getting their subversive jollies from the unsullied effusions of some cow's naked udder.

In the great Puritan tradition of nonconformist worship, our guest had acquired her milk—one of the most highly regulated food substances in the United States—through a secret conventicle of protesting dissenters, a band of lacto-fermentation scofflaws who not only specialized in procuring and distributing unlicensed milk from confidential locations in the outer boroughs, but also sold unpasteurized yogurt, kefir, cream, feta, and cottage cheese. Not to mention some excellent honey.

As it turns out, unpasteurized milk has quite a lot to do with the history of the American stomach. While raw-food celebrants and the deacons of next-wave nutrition may perceive themselves to be at the cutting edge of progressive digestion, they really have much in common with the evil old fanatics from the Massachusetts Bay Colony. The postmodern Puritans focus on banishing all traces of pollution from their digestive tracts and every last antibiotic from all the world's food supply. They believe their gastric system must be perfected, and to hell—quite literally—with anyone who dares interfere. Four companies control almost 85 percent of U.S. fluid-milk sales, so the congregation waits and prays for the day when the behemoths of Big Dairy will lie moldering in the grave, alongside their rotting vats of insulin-spiked recombinant bovine growth hormone (which the raw-foodies call crack for cows). Death to Monsanto, death to ConAgra, and death to the state veterinarians, too!

I knew that in order to understand the forces

that drove American food culture, I would have to infiltrate the ranks of raw-milk worship. Cotton Mather might be long gone, but I could learn quite a bit from his spiritual descendants. Aside from the Puritan twist, I imagined some Prohibition-era frisson to the whole thing, the lost romance of speakeasies, secret passwords, and the sudden terror of steel door smashed to the floor. "New York State Milk Control. Up against the wall!"

"I'd be delighted to take you to the next raw-milk-club coven," our guest from the Midwest e-mailed later that day, "assuming your agenda is not to bust us with New York State Agriculture and Markets, create a massive food scare, and drive some God-fearing Amish farmer into bankruptcy."

I assured her that was not my agenda, so she arranged my electronic introduction to Claudia K., an herbalist, community gardener, and manager of the secret raw-milk-coven LISTSERV. "What kind of a book are you writing?" she wanted to know. And had I heard of a man named Weston A. Price?

A Cleveland dentist born in 1870, Weston Price devoted himself to inspecting the incisors of native populations world round and concluded that the lack of cavities (not to mention lack of jails) among Australian Aborigines, Polynesian South Sea Islanders, Seminole Indians, and Gaels from the Outer Hebrides could be traced to a diet rich in you-know-what. Aside from raw milk, the nonprofit foundation that bears his name advocates plenty of cod-liver oil, lard, and butterfat. It also issues periodic soy studies, soy updates, and soy alerts (the pro-raw-milk crowd and the pro-soy-milk crowd have yet to negotiate a truce).

Raw-milk fanatics abound—from McCordsville, Indiana, to Papaaloa, Hawaii. One Ohio resident swears he drives more than one hundred miles to score his fix. And getting milk straight from a cow to a Manhattan condo has become the latest obsession of urban raw-food disciples, who claim that the unpasteurized stuff works as a "milk cure" for ailments as varied as hypertension, heart disease, stomach cancer, chronic gastritis, eczema, and psoriasis. The East Coast milk crowd disputes accusations (made by the New York State Division of Milk Control and Dairy Services, doctors, biologists, and other dairy-industry stooges) that raw-milk products contain high levels of pathogens that can cause salmonellosis, brucellosis, listeriosis, and tuberculosis.

Of course, none of the raw-food Web sites devotes too much space to a frank discussion of tuberculosis. I did not want to suffer from a disease of any more than four syllables, so I tracked down a Cornell research scientist who explained that two or three million years ago the tuberculin bacteria jumped from the prehistoric muck into the immune cells of mammals, where it hung around to infect and kill scores of ancient Egyptians and ancient Greeks (not to mention Frédéric Chopin, John Keats, and John Harvard). Tuberculosis generally begins to manifest itself as an intestinal infection, the dreaded dyspepsia, origin of all morbidity. Once the stomach has been inflamed, the victim can no longer absorb food and begins to consume himself. Thus: consumption. The victim has a worm in his belly, and it gnaws him! As in anorexia nervosa, the unlucky recipient of a tuberculin-tainted glass of raw milk can end up starving to death. The Centers for Disease Control have reported that more than three hundred raw-milk guzzlers contracted some sort of illness from drinking the white stuff or from eating cheese made from raw milk in 2001, and nearly two hundred became sick from these products in 2002.

There is no cure for tuberculosis. The bacteria can be stabilized but never completely eradicated. Of course, in this country you can believe what you want to believe, particularly when it comes to matters edible and excretable. Leading physicians of the 1840s insisted that a journey across the Santa Fe or Oregon Trail could relieve the suffering of consumptives (not to mention hypochondriacs, dyspeptics, and anyone else suffering from assorted bowel disorders). An army surgeon named Edward Vollum declared that

> the best treatment known for consumption
> was a year of steady, daily horseback-riding

in a mountainous country, and a diet of corn-bread and bacon with a moderate quantity of whiskey.

But I was not convinced.

Almost as long as people have been drinking milk, they have taken it as medicine. The seventeenth-century Swiss physician Johann Jacob Wepfer described a woman who had for many years been afflicted with convulsions and hysterical suffocations. She was cured by drinking milk. And our old friend Cotton Mather trumpeted the near miraculous powers of a milk diet, which

has had wonderful effects in curing many and grievous and such as have been thought incurable ... The use of milk is recommended in a consumption, especially women's milk.

Women's milk? I could not imagine John Winthrop snuggling up to the breast. Of course, it would take a Puritan to articulate the return of our earliest repression. Freudian, Lacanian, and Kleinian readers of this chapter must have immediately concluded that in her desire for purity and intimacy with nature, the raw-milk acolyte searches for a lost nurturer, namely, the absent mother. Thus milk's uncanny powers, as described by generations of pre-Freudian doctors, scientists, and cooks. In her (otherwise) sober and clinical *Food and Cookery for the Sick and Convalescent*, Fannie Farmer recommended "Hydrochloric Milk" as a remedy for typhoid. The recipe: Boil a quart, then lace with twenty-five drops of a 10 percent solution hydrochloric acid.

A few decades before Farmer, the Beecher sisters had commented that "no domestic articles are so sympathetic as those of the milk tribe." The downside of such pervasive sympathies led the Beecher sisters to the brink of "despair as regards bad butter" and the "hobgoblin bewitchment of cream into foul and loathsome poisons":

You turn from your dreadful half-slice of bread, which fills your mouth with bitterness, to your beef-steak, which proves virulent with the same poison; you think to take refuge in vegetable diet, and find the butter in the string-beans, and polluting the innocence of early peas; it is in the corn, in the succotash, in the squash; the beets swim in it, the onions have it poured over them. Hungry and miserable, you think to solace yourself at the dessert; but the pastry is cursed, the cake is acrid with the same plague.

Considering the stakes, it comes as no surprise that the law stepped in.

Cotton Mather and the Beecher sisters had perceived stomach matters as moral issues. But nineteenth-century nutritionist Sylvester Graham took the morality of American consumption to the next level. The depth of his obsession and the popular response his doctrines elicited led Emerson to dub him our "prophet of bran bread and pumpkins."

Fatherless since the age of two, Sylvester Graham had wanted to be a teacher—until sickness derailed this first ambition. Ordained a Presbyterian minister in 1829, Graham soon became an advocate of temperance, and the extreme physical regimen he eventually championed not only proscribed meat but banned liquor, wine, coffee, tea, and tobacco. Above all, Graham believed in the ethical qualities of pure bread, bread created from unsifted and unbolted flour. He scorned the professionally baked varieties with their immoral additives, such as alum and chlorine. Thousands attended his histrionic lectures, which gained credence the more they were threatened by throngs of enraged butchers and bakers.

As a matter of course, Sylvester Graham shunned the pollutions of marketplace milk. And oddly enough (but like many health gurus who came after him, from Adelle Davis to Dr. Atkins), Graham did not live to be old. He was fifty-eight when he succumbed to what his physician cited as a superfluity of warm baths and an overdose of mineral water. Too much purity had proved perilous.

Sylvester Graham preached that we were all God's children, but he transformed this standard spiritual metaphor into a matter of digestive grace. "Treat your stomach like a well-governed child," he advised.

> Carefully find out what is best for it, as the digestive organ of your body, and then teach it to conform to your regimen, and soon its habitude will become what is commonly called nature.
> ... "Whatever pleases the palate, must agree with the stomach and nourish the body!" This lying proverb is older than the Christian Religion, and has sent millions of human beings thro' years of misery to an early grave.... But let it ever be remembered that the palate may be educated to any thing ...

Just as the Old Testament prophets declared that we must circumcise our heart for God, Sylvester Graham declared that we must discipline our stomach for society. To be explicit, Graham viewed hunger as a dangerous erection of the digestive apparatus. He lectured on sexual abstinence as often as he lectured on diet reform, advocated cold showers, and warned against the manifold perils of onanism. Like the Founding Fathers, Graham perceived that the greatest enemy of representative democracy was unchecked passion (which could lead to the dangers of mobocracy), and since the digestive tract was the

seat of all passion, Graham's faith-based diet of seda-
tive whole grains promised to be an antidote to the
appalling convulsions of an increasingly industrial-
ized and economically polarized America. For
Sylvester Graham, the ultimate goal was social—a
strictly hygienic country made up of hardworking,
God-fearing, gluten-munching, anesthetized celibates.

Instead of ostracizing him for being the wacko
he was, citizens became enthusiastic about Graham's
regimen; they signed up in droves, and the ranks of
his followers came to include such legendary American moralists as Henry David Thoreau, who followed a modified Grahamite regimen during his
years cultivating beans at Walden Pond.

History has clarified the forces that led Graham
to his obsession with the ethics of eating, and
America to its obsession with Graham. Inventories
from the age of Jackson indicate that even rural
families had begun to consume luxury food items,
including such relished excitements as mustard, cinnamon, ginger, raisins, chocolate, Madeira, salted
herring, and "peppersauce." Most sinister of all
Jacksonian grocery-buying habits was the fact that
probate records indicate households were no longer
storing as much corn and rye as they had a century
before. Instead of stocking their basements with
amber waves of grain, families had begun to consume store-bought bread.

Graham's response to depraved loaves has
stayed with us. The anti–Wonder Bread syndrome

remains a way for Americans to combat their impotence in the face of commercialism, a way to ensure their bodily and spiritual purity, and a great way to act out their paranoia. Retail bakers' loaves had been "drugged with ammonia and other disagreeable things," declared the reform-minded Beecher sisters; but the true housewife, they affirmed, "makes her bread the sovereign of her kitchen":

> The snowy mass, perfectly mixed, kneaded with care and strength, rises in its beautiful perfection till the moment comes for filling the air cells by baking. A few minutes now, and the acetous fermentation will begin, and the whole result be spoiled. Many breadmakers pass in utter carelessness over this sacred and mysterious boundary.

"The best bread in the world," confirmed nineteenth-century diet reformer William Alcott,

> is that which is made of recently and coarsely ground wheat meal, mixed with water, and baked in thin cakes, not unlike the unfermented cakes ... so much used by the ancient Israelites.

And so, declared the Beecher sisters,

> We earnestly entreat American housekeepers, in scriptural language, to stand in the way and

ask for the old paths, and return to the good yeast-bread of their sainted grandmothers.

Who among the old gastrosophers could have predicted that one day in the dim future, the vast proportion of modern industrial U.S. food production would strictly adhere to standards straight from the Bible?

If there is one central idea that unites today's food obsessives with those of our past, it is this: What you eat must be pure and holy. But what does "pure and holy" mean? The most commonly accepted answer is that "pure and holy" means kosher, the restrictions specifically laid out in the third and fifth books of the Torah. Paramount among these dietary prohibitions stands the taboo against mixing milk and meat (no kosher cheeseburgers).

Some argue that milk to the Old Testament Hebrew symbolized life itself; thus, it must never be mixed with defunct flesh, the essence of death (Thou shalt not seethe a kid in his mother's milk). But there are those who counter that the Old Testament's dietary laws were politically motivated, a matter of suppressing the influence of other ancient Canaanite tribes, for whom boiling meat in mother's milk was a cultic act. Others assert that the abomination of all creeping things was stolen straight from Zoroastrianism, while many believe the dietary rules were purposefully made to be arbitrary and irrational, discipline for the sake of discipline. The ancient philosopher Philo thought that kosher was simply a matter of choosing the most delicious cuts of meat, although anyone who has ever devoured a platter of pork fried rice has grounds to debate Philo. Hygiene, too, has long been a popular theory—that pig has trichinosis! But it turns out hygiene has little if nothing to do with kosher. A dinner of Three Cheese Pizza Bagels with Ice Cream Classic Cake Log for dessert may be kosher, but no nutrition guru on earth would dare call it healthy.

In a country where physical health and spiritual health have both been associated with economic health, kosher has underscored its purity and godliness by its cash value. Today in the United States it is hard to avoid eating food that some rabbi, somewhere, has not certified kosher. Market specialists now assert that out of a $500 billion grocery market, U.S. food manufacturers sell more than $170 billion worth of kosher-certified products each year. Whenever a company takes a food line kosher, it sees a jump in American market share. And for Nestlé or Nabisco or Best Foods or General Mills, even a fraction of a percentage point may translate into millions of dollars.

According to *U.S. News & World Report*, 28 percent of Americans say they have knowingly purchased a kosher product in the past year; and only 8 percent of those did so for religious reasons. Kosher may be a myth, chuckle Heinz and Pillsbury, but it's our kind of myth. A myth that increases sales. Because it's not only observant Jews who eat kosher—it's Muslims and Seventh-Day Adventists, throngs of the lactose intolerant, vegetarians and the health conscious, and even those who believe kosher adds a little ethnic spritz to the table. Of course, the slow-food and the pure-food and the raw-food crowd like kosher, too.

Health was not the God of Abraham, Isaac, and Jacob; health is the American God. So the revisionist logic runs something like this: Since God is health, all that God approves must be healthy. Kosher is approved by God; therefore, kosher is healthy. Result of the syllogism? Here in the land of the gluten-free, "Certified Kosher" has joined "Organic," "All Natural," and "No Preservatives" at the very top of Mount Sinai. It's the same kind of thinking that led my guest to raw-milk obsession, only on a much, much larger scale.

Kosher got its start in the New World in New Amsterdam in 1656, when twenty-three Sephardic refugees got off the boat and Asser Levy, "the Jew butcher," became one of the city's first official meat cleavers (recall that back in the 1650s, butchers had to be sworn in—like the president or a Supreme Court judge). Within one hundred years, Levy's spiritual and culinary descendants would be exporting New York kosher beef to Jamaica and Curaçao, while Jewish would-be fur traders and frontiersmen packed up their supplies of roast herring, kosher sausage, and hard-boiled eggs—and headed west.

Dr. Brown's famous celery soda (Cel-Ray) made its debut in 1869, and Fleischmann's kosher yeast appeared on the market the following year. Dov Behr Manischewitz's turn-of-the-century matzo machine produced fifty thousand pounds of unleavened bread a day, and he sold them all. Isaac Breakstone set up his butter works in the 1880s, and Isadore Pinckowitz began producing kosher frankfurters in 1905 (an operation that would eventually become Hebrew National, before being swallowed by ConAgra).

In 1911 Procter & Gamble invented Crisco, a vegetable-based shortening created from hydrogenated cottonseed oil. Before the advent of vegetable-based fat, kosher cooks had only meat-based fats or chicken schmaltz at their disposal, which put a severe crimp in their baking style. (Like raw vegetables, vegetable shortening was neutral, partaking of neither milk nor meat.) Crisco's 1912 marketing campaign touted its newfangled fat as the redemption for which the "Hebrew race has been waiting 4,000 years."

Pillsbury, Borden, Mazola, and Maxwell House (which had introduced the world's first kosher-for-Passover coffee) soon fashioned their own kosher print campaigns, and by 1912 Macy's was running full-page ads for its kosher honey, kosher almonds, kosher ginger, and kosher California prunes. In 1935

Heinz baked beans went kosher. In 1937 so did Coca-Cola.

Today Wal-Mart sells kosher products, along with Trader Joe's and Whole Foods and FreshDirect and A&P and Safeway. In fact, the average American supermarket carries thirteen thousand products approved by God. And kosher economics do trickle down. One level beneath the retail kosher product lurks the wholesale kosher ingredient. And beneath the ingredient lies the infinitely recursive level of the ingredients of the ingredients, the substances of the substances, which are themselves combinations of even more basic substances. There is plenty of purity and spirituality and profit to go around, even on the esoteric strata of emulsifiers, flavor enhancers, starches, and dehydrates. Here, in the land of ascorbic acid, dextrose, and ethyl vanillin, the market saturation of products certified kosher reaches an overwhelming 80 percent. If you take into consideration that some ingredients will never be kosher, no matter what (essence of fried pork rind comes to mind), that 80 percent figure, in real terms, means that 100 percent of the food substance in America that could be kosher is, in fact, kosher. God bless America.

Now consider that a single bite of a Frito-Lay brand certified-kosher barbecue-flavored potato chip delivers dehydrated starch from Idaho, dehydrated onions from China, dehydrated garlic from India, and a bit of paprika from Spain, all of which must be certified kosher. "A simple product has ten, twenty ingredients," explained one of the throng of rabbis I met at a yearly trade show called Kosherfest. "Twenty certifications behind the certification, you see? I don't think anyone understands the globalization of the food market as we do."

Indeed. The holiness of the American gut recognizes no border. Every day the tally of rootless cosmopolitan kosher certifiers grows: Just as Rabbi Benjamin Papermaster immigrated from Lithuania in 1890 to prepare kosher meat for the Jews of North Dakota, Shimon Freudlich, a Chabad rabbi, now lives in Beijing. Shalom Greenberg has moved to Shanghai. Moshe Gutnick works out of Australia, Yosef Kantor from Thailand. These mashgiachs can walk into any factory on earth, interview the chief of R & D, apply their expertise in chemistry, food technology, and the laws of Deuteronomy and Leviticus, then rule. All to supply the American food chain.

When it comes to stomachs, the biggest secret of all is the enzyme. What has been brutalized in pasteurized milk? According to the raw-milk .coms and .orgs, the mental, spiritual, and physical benefits of "real" milk not only derive from mother lodes of vitamins and flora but from more than sixty different exquisite and unreplicable enzymes hidden within the fat globules and somatic cells, enzymes that are routinely annihilated by the high pressure and high heat (generally 15 to 20 seconds at 161.5 degrees Fahrenheit) of Louis Pasteur's 1862 process. It is the possibility of ingesting the rare jewel of a raw-milk enzyme that drives the lacto gang to their extremes. Enzymes are the Holy Ghost of holy food. They are powerful, they are mysterious, but no one I spoke to could answer the basic question: What's an enzyme?

When it comes to producing food, enzymes are nothing new. In *The Odyssey*, Homer describes how after milking his goat, the Cyclops Polyphemus

> took half the cheese, which he skillfully curdled, separated from the whey, and stowed in wicker baskets.

Polyphemus knew how to make cheese because he knew how to use an ancient enzyme called rennet, a protein that can be scraped from the stomach lining of suckling calves.

In 1830 diet guru Lydia Maria Child advocated a blood-warm mixture of wine and milk curdled with "rennet-water" as a cure for fevers. And rennet remained on America's medicine shelf. "Rennets properly prepared and dried, are sold constantly in the Philadelphia markets," Miss Leslie remarked a decade after Lydia Child.

> The cost is trifling; and it is well to have one always in the house, in case of being wanted

to make whey for sick persons. They will keep a year or more.

In fact, calves aren't the only ones with enzymes in their bellies. In 1822 an accidental shooting left a young French Canadian mountie named Alexis St. Martin with a permanent gastric fistula—a long, sinuous, pipelike ulcer that led from the outside of St. Martin's body to the inside of his stomach. An American frontier doctor named William Beaumont saw his opportunity to unveil the "powers of the gastric organs," and was soon suspending

flesh, raw and roasted, and other substances in the hole, to ascertain the length of time required to digest each.

Thus did Beaumont beat English and Continental physiologists in the race to discover the biochemical processes of digestion. Thus did Beaumont discover enzymes in the American gut.

Today books like *Enzyme Nutrition,* *The Enzyme Cure,* and *The Complete Book of Enzyme Therapy* acknowledge the pivotal role of enzymes in the strange transformations of whatever it is you eat for dinner into the energy it takes to do the dishes. We may debate whether or not the key to American identity lies within the history of the American stomach, but the key to American digestion cannot be argued: It is the enzyme.

And there's money in those molecules. Designer enzymes have become the darling of American packaged-food producers because they can do anything artificial ingredients can do, and more: bind, stabilize, sweeten, coagulate, clarify, dissolve, foam, tenderize, and texturize. They can increase crumb quality, enhance aroma, and improve sliceability and what people in the food business call "mouthfeel." But there is one enormous difference between an enzyme and an artificial ingredient: Enzymes do not have to be listed on the ingredient panel.

Before the ice cream (raw-milk or not) or dehydrated gravy (kosher or not) has reached its final state as a packaged product, the enzymes that created the comestible have disappeared. They have, quite literally, become ghosts in the food-production machine. The enzymes are like coaches or lobbyists—enablers of processes that, in the end, they do not execute. Thus can the ingredient panel of the kosher-certified, all-natural, organic loaf of whole-grain wheat bread become the fantasy of every retailer: flour, water, salt—and nothing else. Since enzymes are "recovered" after they have been used, there's no need to list the Fungamyl, the Novamyl, the Pentopan, the Gluzyme, the Lipopan, and all the other various and sundry gene-shuffled proteins that have increased the loaf volume of almost every hot-dog and hamburger bun sold in America today. By the time the buns hit the supermarket shelves, the enzymes have moved on to English muffins.

In 1869 the Beecher sisters had declared that truly spiritual bread must be "light, sweet, and tender," and further noted that "this matter of lightness is the distinctive line between savage and civilized bread." Today mass-produced designer enzymes not only sanctify our daily bread with the light of civilization, they bless the loaf with longer shelf life, better water retention, a browner crust, superior dough handling, stability, tolerance, and machinability. And then they go away. It's a miracle, the uncanny convergence of fairies and microbiology: Frankenfood that vanishes without a trace. Awe-inspiring, numinous, and salvific, enzymes are perhaps most reminiscent of that bush that burned with fire but was not consumed.

Which brings us back to Jehovah: In order for the packaged yogurt or marinade or baby food to be certified pure and godlike (i.e., kosher), all its ingredients must be certified pure and godlike (i.e., ditto); and in order for the ingredients to be certified kosher, the enzymes that have mediated the creation of said ingredients must, in turn, be certified kosher. And in order for an enzyme to be certified kosher, that enzyme must keep kosher. And who ensures that the enzymes keep kosher? That's right. It's a mashgiach.

One rabbi described an urgent call from a start-up biotech company that had come up with a new strain of some wonder genetically modified organism, a protein that would accelerate cheese ripening or extract a more savory meat flavor from scrap-bone residue. The tech-savvy certifier had been deployed on an emergency basis to check that the new microorganism was kosher, only to find that the infant enzyme cultures—which, like any newborn, require a rich diet—had been nourished on a substrate of brain tissue and an infusion of pig heart, with a little human blood serum on top. Definitely not kosher.

What to do? Try to feed the germs something else, of course. But what if those itty-bitty bacterial colonies get finicky? They like their human blood serum. They don't want kosher potato flakes! They don't want boiled beets and carrots! They don't want soya grits or V8 Juice (a common starter for colonies of gene-mutated enzymes).

At this point the rabbis in New York get the call and the halachic heavy hitters convene in conference rooms lined with Torah, Talmud, and the commentaries. One Orthodox Union certifier told me that the rabbinic experts there spend more time on biotech than anything else. And kosher rulings involve some of the most nuanced and complicated of all rabbinic interpretations. Perhaps if the baby GMO subsides primarily on pulverized potato flakes, it might qualify. But given the inherent complexities, there are no straightforward judgments. Here, the Orthodox Union must determine, in essence, whether the feed media for the enzyme is kosherish.

Pushed to the extremes of serving the American

stomach, the solemn edicts of Leviticus and Deuteronomy must make their peace with the demigods of modern biotechnology.

When I returned from my excursions into kosherland, I found urgent news about the secret raw-milk drop-off. An e-mail included thanks for my interest in nonindustrialized food, a price list ($4.25 per gallon of raw milk, $4.00 for a quart of raw cottage cheese), the location of the drop-off site, and a downloadable contract. ("It's unenforceable," my lawyer declared, but I signed it anyway.)

One week later, on a cold winter night, I entered the basement of a large apartment building in Hell's Kitchen. Manhattan's first-ever covert market in raw milk was about to open, and I introduced myself to Claudia K., who introduced me to everybody else. Which was how I met Nathan Donohoe, a massage therapist and student of organic cooking.

"These guys are saving people's lives," Donohoe said as he helped set up the tables. "I was allergic to milk for ten years. But I found out if I have raw milk, I can drink as much as I want." In addition to his milk allergy, Donohoe related a baroque history of ailments, including attention deficit disorder, bipolar disorder, and chronic fatigue syndrome. "I started raw milk only a month ago," he said. "But I feel incredible."

By 6:15 P.M. the coven members had begun to show up, greeting each other with silent nods. They

eyed strangers with suspicion. Were they soy
drinkers? One rumor had it that an angry vegan
might be infiltrating the ranks. I had heard of these
hard-core, tattooed, macho-punk almond-chewers,
and while no one of that description mingled with
the crowd, fear persisted. "All you need is one person in the dairy world to tell someone else," warned
Claudia K.

At precisely 6:30 the coolers were opened, re-
vealing a tightly packed stash of bootleg milk, butter,
cream cheese, and glistening white feta (any unpasteurized cheese aged less than sixty days is highly regulated by New York's Milk Control Board).

A farmer named Vernon, baby-faced and
dressed in black jeans, began stuffing brown paper
bags with his goods. His customers included a
painter, a sculptor, a violinist, a computer program-
mer, an eyeglass salesman, a few stay-at-home moms,
some neighborhood activists, a little girl in a
princess costume, and a rather preppy couple, Mary
Serrilli and her husband, Eric, who sported a con-
servative blue blazer.

"We're gonna do shots of whey!" Mary said. "A
shot of whey a day!"

I did not tell the Serrillis that Cotton Mather
himself was a great advocate of whey, not only
"plentifully drank," but "injected by clysters."
Whey, declared Mather,

> is of considerable virtue. Several authors
> count it a great anti-dysenteric arcanum.

Whatever that meant. Behind the Serrillis stood a thin, frizzy-haired woman named Jo-Jo. "I'm a canine nutritionist," she told me. When one of Jo-Jo's dogs developed colitis, she started feeding it raw milk, saw health improvements, then went raw herself. "Kibble is a dead food."

Wayne Burkey, a residential real-estate broker at Sotheby's, lives in Tribeca with his wife and two-year-old twins. "I don't consume any of this," he whispered as he loaded his stash into a folding grocery cart. He said that he had eaten a banana and had consumed three cups of coffee for breakfast that morning, and admitted to liking hot dogs. "We do this for the children," he said. "They've never been sick. Not even a cold."

A Dominican-born dog walker named Danny Polanco articulated the Marxist-Leninist-Sylvester Grahamite perspective. "This is a challenge to the commodification of life itself," he declared, then added that he regularly ingests raw animal foods, such as cow hearts. "I clean off any arteries, cut it into small pieces, and I eat it."

"No marinade?" a coven member asked. "No mustard?"

"I just cut it up," Polanco said. "I'm a minimalist."

After an hour of hushed transactions, Claudia K. was getting tired. "I am spending so much of my life for this," she said. "Sometimes I think, *What am I doing it for?*" But she quickly recovered. "It's worth it. It creates a community. It's really wonderful to have real food."

Then she lowered her voice. "The thing I am most protective about is the farmer." She looked over at Vernon, who was doing just fine. His supply had sold out, and he was packing up the empty coolers, his pocket stuffed with crumpled checks and thick wads of cash.

I climbed the basement stairs, my brown-paper bag of underground milk and Amish honey tucked under an arm, and headed uptown to my dinner reservation (Jean Georges, for some transcendental trout sashimi with lemon foam, celestial sea scallops with caper-raisin emulsion, and a dose of enzyme-jacked foie-gras brûlée for dessert). In the land of milk and honey I had the milk, and I had the honey. I was one of the Elect, and despite the cold I grinned at yet another victory for the American gut, holy of holies, spirit in the flesh. But as the taxis splattered and my writerly tweeds grew damp and heavy, a chill took hold and I couldn't help fearing that deep within the purity and whiteness lay a budding flower of tuberculin, a bosom serpent waiting to unleash destruction.

4

Manifest Dinner

Like as a mighty alderman, when at a corporation feast the first spoonful of turtle soup salutes his palate, feels his impatient appetite but ten-fold quickened, and re-doubles his vigorous attacks upon the tureen, while his voracious eyes, projecting from his head, roll greedily round devouring every thing at table—so did the mettle-some Peter Stuyvesant, feel that intolerable hunger for martial glory, which raged within his very bowels.

—Washington Irving, 1809

A few days before I traveled to Plymouth to gaze at the Rock and partake in a Pilgrim harvest dinner reenactment ($54.95 a person, and Miller Lites for $4.50), I traveled to midtown Manhattan to witness the inaugural Thanksgiving Meal Invitational competitive-eating contest, a particularly gruesome event in which the top seven professional gurgitators in America had been invited to consume as much turkey and all the fixings as was humanly possible in twelve minutes.

Over the past several years, front-page stories

have appeared in the *Wall Street Journal* and the *Los Angeles Times*, books have been published about the phenomena, and when Eric Booker set the new world record in matzo balls (twenty-one in five minutes), it made the CNN news crawl; when MTV's *True Life* "I'm a Competitive Eater" episode aired in February of 2006, it doubled the network's prime-time average. ESPN recently purchased exclusive rights to the July Fourth hot-dog-eating contest, and they broadcast the bratwurst event, too.

Of course, competitive eating has long transcended hot dogs. Disciplines now include chicken wings in Philadelphia (a contest that draws a live audience in excess of twenty thousand), jalapeños in Laredo, crawfish in Baton Rouge, oysters in New Orleans, conch fritters in Key West, and chili in Reno. Not since the glory days of goldfish swallowing has the sport annexed such a large portion of the country's collective delirium. And so the International Federation of Competitive Eating (IFOCE) sanctions a gamut of increasingly baroque competitions in fields such as Tater Tots, sticks of butter, cow brains, and straight mayonnaise.

"There's a reverence for this as history," said George Shea, founder of the IFOCE. Indeed, the first published report of an American competitive-eating contest appeared on May 29, 1786, in the *New York Gazette*:

Yesterday, a countryman in the Fly Market, for a trifling wager, ate fifty boiled eggs, shells and all. He performed the task in about fifteen minutes, being elevated on a butcher's block during the operation. . . .

As Walt Whitman would declare a half-dozen decades later, the American must contain multitudes. One of the most obvious roads to such multitudinous containment has passed through the stomach, from whence it emerged as the eating mythologies of Davy Crockett, Paul Bunyan, and all those other frontier roarers, screamers, and savage Mississippi boatmen who, according to no less an authority than Mark Twain, ate a dozen eggs for breakfast each morning, shell and all, and never once suffered indigestion.

Add to the fastings and pukes of our Puritan ancestors the sheer abundance of the new continent and the geographical opportunities for expansion, and the result was an obsession with physical control and consumption on a scale the world had never before seen. The center of our medicine and the Main Digester of our spiritual life, the American stomach soon came to engulf our political ideas. Call it imperialist eating.

When I arrived at the Thanksgiving contest, my attention first settled on the man who was at the time renowned as the greatest of all American eaters, Eric "Badlands" Booker (6′6″, 460 pounds). Booker has a sweet smile and a gentle disposition and has held world records in hard-boiled eggs (thirty-eight in eight minutes, no shells), burritos (fifteen in eight minutes), onions, candy bars, doughnuts, peas, pumpkin pie, and hamentaschen (fifty traditional Purim cookies in six minutes). I edged into the media scrum and heard the standard questions about bird-eating strategy, and I dutifully recorded Booker's charming answers.

"I strive to better myself in eating," Booker told the cameras and the pencils. "Every year I'm increasing my capacity, increasing my speed. Just like John Henry did on the railroad. John Henry was a big guy, a black man, a strong man," said Booker. "He built the railroad. I do that in a certain way. I'm in that environment."

John Henry, the steel-driving American legend, had confronted his country's unquenchable desire to consume space and compress time and as a direct result hammered railroad ties until he collapsed and died. Eric "Badlands" Booker, confronting his own version of the American need to possess and expand and control, had eaten himself into a roomful of trophies, a "Badlands" Booker Web site, a collection of video clips, freezers full of frozen hot dogs (which is what you get for winning hot-dog-eating contests), and a heady dose of fame. Booker has featured prominently in the two extant books about competitive eating, has been the subject of a profile in *Sports Illustrated*, has appeared in numerous magazine articles and on dozens of television shows, and has been quoted in countless newspaper articles. He has become famous for what he eats and the way he eats it. Millions of Americans have been struck with admiration and disgust—as though Eric Booker were a throwback to the time of the wild frontier, as if he were the master of the untamed (if eponymous) badlands, an object of awe and fear. Someone like John Henry or Daniel Boone.

A week earlier I had accompanied Eric Booker as he conducted his train. No, it was not John Henry's C&O Railroad; not a train packed with pigs and printing presses, headed west through the plains; not the Union Pacific or the Southern Pacific or even Amtrak. Eric Booker's train was a subway, the No. 7 Flushing line that runs from Times Square to Shea Stadium and back.

In the middle of the ride came the moment of enlightenment: When the train emerged in Queens, it rose from underground to tower above the borough on a great swerving track, and I watched as one of the most profound digesters in American history looked down from on high to the enormous, edible polyglot that crowded every square block of this county: Chinese noodle shops, Argentinean steak houses, Indian curry houses, Mexican taquerías, Cypriot lunch counters, Chino-Latino, cuchifrito. . . . How had such a thing happened? I asked myself. How had America digested the world?

That same question crashed through my mind as I stood amid the crowd at the Thanksgiving contest.

And as the press skirmished for front-row seats, I could not stop thinking about John Henry and the railroads, American imperialism, and Manifest Destiny. If legendary Americans possessed legendary guts, what could their mythic ingestions tell us about American aspirations and anxieties? What could our heroes and antiheroes reveal about our stomachs, ourselves? The notes I began to scribble had nothing to do with eating contests, and when I finally looked up I saw a large man in a coonskin cap. At first I thought it was a hallucination; then I realized it was Dale Boone.

I had not considered the case of Dale Boone until then, but there he was, "The Mouth from the South" in his signature outfit: freshly ironed bib overalls, shiny shit-kicking boots, and that coonskin cap. He certainly had the pedigree of a legend. Son of Otto Jack, son of Hudson Daniel, son of James Andrew Jackson, son of Robert Nelson, son of James Andrew, son of Jeremiah, son of Thomas, son of Jonathan . . . son of Daniel Boone.

"I'm the ninth descendant down!" Boone was hollering to anyone within earshot. Boone, six feet tall and 280 pounds, strutted around Mickey Mantle's restaurant, pausing only to jawbone the TV crews or pose for snapshots. I knew he held eating titles in reindeer sausage (28 in ten minutes), Russian beef dumplings (274 in six minutes), and pork and beans (84 ounces of baked beans in one minute, fifty-two seconds). The night before, Boone had prepped himself: boiled cabbage, turnip greens, carrots, corn, nothing heavy. Now his stomach was stretched and ready. "Yeeeeeee-haw!" he cried. "This is the best I've felt in a long time."

Ever since he was a little boy, everyone had told him to slow down and taste his food. Everyone, that is, except his uncle. Daniel Homer Boone was a tremendous eater, so thorough and unmerciful in his feedings that he was banned from several buffets in Asheville, North Carolina. Daniel Homer Boone measured six feet eleven inches tall and weighed 435 pounds. His wife, on the other hand, was one inch shy of four feet. Young Dale Boone was the only person who could keep up with his uncle.

> Multitudes, in this country of abundance, are trained from their veriest infancy to eat three or four times as much as they ought,

noted the nineteenth-century gastrosophist William Alcott; trained, Alcott continued, to distend their stomachs enormously. Alcott concluded,

> it is he who labors, thinks, recreates himself, and sleeps in the most just proportion, who can eat the most food.

Watermelon had been Dale Boone's first attempt, at the annual Locust Grove Day in Locust Grove,

Georgia. Grand prize: a six-pack of Coca-Cola. The year was 1991, and Dale Boone had graduated from Georgia Tech with a degree in electrical engineering. He was just beginning his journey to re-create himself as a modern American digestive legend (laboring, thinking, and sleeping in the most just proportion)—and he lost to a twelve-year-old. "It got me going," said Boone. "I had to come back and prove myself the next year and the next year."

Dale Boone believes he reached peak eating speeds at twenty-one, and he won whatever-could-be-put-on-a-plate eating contests in and around Atlanta until he retired from stunt eating, married, opened his own business, and became a vegetarian.

But just as the pioneer Daniel Boone abandoned domesticated life to settle ever newer territories, the gurgitator Dale Boone could not deny the imperatives of his roving metabolism. In April 2002 Atlanta's AM 790, "The Zone," announced three eating contests in a single day: doughnuts in the morning, pigs' feet in the afternoon, chicken wings at night. Dale Boone had made no conscious decision to come out of retirement. Still, it was inevitable that on the day of the contest "The Mouth from the South" would somehow, someway, be impelled to the broadcast studio. Once there Dale Boone devastated a dozen Krispy Kremes in two minutes, walked away with the prize, and that afternoon returned for contest number two.

"It was one pig's foot and sixteen ounces of very

sour buttermilk. Next thing I know, contest started, bang! It took me nine seconds. Nine seconds!"

After two straight wins, Boone had to hang around for the hot wings. He knew he could eat faster than anyone else in the state and wasn't the least bit intimidated by the 350-pounder from the University of Georgia who rolled into the studio. Dale Boone was swallowing number twenty-nine while the opposition was still gnawing number five. "The hot sauce was hitting him," Boone reminisced. "His face was like five or six shades of red. I took the last one, I wiggled it in his face. I said, 'Come on, fat boy,' and then just finished it off and threw it down." Dale Boone thus became the undisputed AM-radio champion eater of Atlanta.

Still, he was not satisfied. He had heard of other eating contests, brimming tables beyond the borders of Georgia and the Carolinas. Deep in his guts, Dale Boone knew the frontier was still out there, waiting to be conquered.

Our first grocers were the natives, who provided deer and bird flesh in the winter, fish in the summer, and a never-ending cycle of maize, known simply as Indian. Just as we eat Chinese today, the early Americans ate Indian, and the metonymy persisted into the twentieth century, when in her *Food and Cookery for the Sick and Convalescent*, Fannie Farmer lauded Indian mixed with warm water as a gentle laxative.

"Put the Indian in your bread-pan," cookbook author Lydia Maria Child advised in 1832. But be sure to have enough hot water on hand: "Indian absorbs a great deal of water."

By 1840 the country's most popular cookbook—Miss Eliza Leslie's *Directions for Cookery*—had recast the homegrown American subsistence into such haute hybrids as Indian bread, Indian flapjacks, Indian muffins, baked Indian pudding (with grated lemon peel), boiled Indian pudding (to be savored with wine sauce), Indian pudding without eggs (but with plenty of cinnamon and butter), Indian dumplings (boiled in cheesecloth), Indian pound cake (add powdered white sugar, a glass of white wine, and a glass of brandy), Indian batter cake, and even a proper Boston Indian mush. Of course, such refinements sugarcoated a history rife with violence. At some point in this country's strange story, taking a bite and wielding a weapon had become equivalent acts—Indian chief and Indian mush faced similar fates.

In 1637 a force of ninety men led by Captain John Mason prepared to march from Hartford to Saybrook to battle the Pequots. Before they set off, the renowned Puritan reverend Thomas Hooker preached that the Pequots should be bread for them, a metaphor that neatly summed up the arc of the Native American from grocer to grocery. And when the severed head of the dreaded sachem King Philip was finally brought into Plymouth, the great congregationalist divine Cotton Mather praised

God for providing meat to the people inhabiting the wilderness. (While the merely evil Native Americans became the metaphorical equivalent of manna, the unquestionably satanic Quakers merited the ultimate Puritan opprobrium. According to Mather, they were nothing less than "the vomit cast out in the by-past ages . . . lick'd up again for a new digestion.") Even a food as seemingly innocuous as gingerbread was in its original American incarnation the substance of an exercise in imperialist eating. A military ration, gingerbread was used to refresh the troops on morning musters, and on one memorable day in March 1711, the troops ate nothing but gingerbread in a display of strength intended to intimidate a band of Tuscarora Indians.

The original version of "Yankee Doodle" was not so much about patriotism as it was about eating Indian:

> *Husking time is coming on.*
> *They all begin to laugh sir—*
> *Father is a coming home*
> *To kill the heifer calf sir.*
>
> *Corn Cobs twist your hair,*
> *Cart wheel run round you,*
> *Fiery dragons take you off,*
> *And mortal pestal pound you.*
>
> *Now husking time is over*
> *They have a duced frolic.*

> *There'll be some as drunk as sots,*
> *The rest will have the cholic.*

Before he battled the British, Yankee Doodle was a beef-eating, corn-swilling drunkard who was also quite fond of that other Native American edible oddity—the squash called pumpkin:

> *My Mammy, when she carried me,*
> *Dream'd of a wondrous something,—*
> *She dream'd she bore a great Mushroom,*
> *As large as any Pumpkin.*

> *O then a great man will be I,*
> *And all my Foes be worsted;*
> *I'll be a Lord,—and Pumpkin Pie*
> *Devour until I'm bursted.*

Thus did edible Indian become as American as apple pie. Thus did the Yankee frontiersman spring forth as an eater of the most vicious persuasion.

We say we are appalled by the spectacle of worm-crunching reality TV contestants; horrified by cow-brain-bolting competitive eaters; repulsed by the biannual "Phylum Party" hosted by the Biology Department of Rhode Island College, where students feast on snail salad garnished with grasshoppers, mealworms, and crickets. But the American stomach remains mesmerized by such taboo food. Our fascination with extreme eating marks the return of the repressed.

What have we repressed? The fact that in the beginning, the boundaries had been broken. That fact that, here, it was finally possible to eat anything. In 1609 Henry Hudson sat down with some upstate Wappingers for a solemn feast of fatted dog. A bit farther south, the Lenapes were kind enough to share their raccoon and lynx, which they gobbled raw. Taken captive by the Narragansetts in 1676, Mary Rowlandson reported that the Indians

> would pick up old bones, and cut them to pieces at the joints, and if they were full of worms and maggots, they would scald them over the fire to make the vermin come out; and then boil them, and drink up the liquor. . . . They would eat horses guts and ears, and all sorts of wild birds which they could catch: Also bear, venison, beavers, tortoise, frogs, squirrels, dogs, skunks, rattlesnakes: yea, the very barks of trees.

Revolted at the outset of her journey, within a week Rowlandson was herself bolting pancakes fried in bear grease, slurping horse-foot stew, munching deer fetus, and rooting for acorns and groundnuts. Once, when the poor, starving captive tasted broiled horse intestine and found her spirits revived, she quoted the book of Samuel 14:29: "Mine eyes have been enlightened, because I tasted a little of this honey."

In 1759 J. Hector St. John de Crèvecoeur disembarked in the port of New York. He became a surveyor, a trader, a traveler, a farmer, a spy, and by the time he returned to France he had become an expert in all things American. After the American Revolution, his opus, *Letters from an American Farmer*, noted that the earliest frontiersmen were "no better than carnivorous animals of a superior rank, living on the flesh of wild animals when they can catch them." Such eating habits tended "to alter their temper."

In 1789 renowned Methodist John Wesley noted cases of "Canine Appetite." Luckily, back in those days an "insatiable desire of eating" had a cure: "a small bit of bread dipped in wine, and applied to the nostrils." A French traveler named Constantin Volney argued that savage American feasting ruined the Yankee stomach, destroyed the teeth, and extinguished health. And in 1804 yet another repulsed French food tourist noted the following national characteristic: "They swallow almost without chewing."

The American was understood to be a new man—and a new woman—who could partake of the most barbarous aliment. Consider our native wild turkeys, which were large, heavy, fat, and fine, noted the Dutchman Van der Donk, "weighing from twenty to thirty pounds each." Such amazing assertions guaranteed that some of the earliest visitors to this country would be natural scientists, come to marvel at the astounding size and bizarre variety of American food. Some of these researchers became our first food experts, and their conflation of eating and science set a pattern that remains with us.

An explorer named John Bartram traversed more than a thousand miles of wilderness in 1738, collecting forest seeds, sending boxes of turtle eggs to his friends, and feasting on gargantuan persimmons. A Swedish taxonomist named Pehr Kalm sent detailed reports home about such marvels as corn, beans, and the stunning phenomenon of a forty-seven-pound watermelon. Most famous of all, Jean Anthelme Brillat-Savarin, author of *The Physiology of Taste*, journeyed through the wilds of Connecticut in search of the authentic American repast.

None left disappointed. After all, it was here that the Puritan John Winthrop reported more than ten thousand pigeons in a flock. It was here that in the spring of 1754, so many pigeons glutted the New York markets that a buyer could purchase six for a penny, which was a good deal even then. As late as 1858 a Michigan hunter could snare 648 with a single haul of a bird net.

One of the first settlers of New Amsterdam had raised his musket and with a mighty blast downed eleven gray geese. And from that moment to the middle of the nineteenth century, the variety of fowl for sale in New York could not be surpassed by any other market in the world. If a shopper wanted

duck for dinner, there were eighteen types to choose
from—including skunk duck, velvet duck, and
squaw duck.

Behind the duck stood row upon row of
butchered swans, geese, pelicans, widgeons, loons,
broadbills, teals, goosanders, grebes, coots, and
spoonbills. And of course there was woodcock, generally considered the most delicate eating of all the
birds known. And then there were the cormorants,
the robins, the blue jays, and the woodpeckers.

The waters were as wondrous as the land.
Clearly struck by a case of American eating mania,
Pehr Kalm devoured dolphin and reported it "palat-
able food, but rather sometimes dry." Three decades
later the *New York Weekly Post Boy* reported that a
certain Bernard Johnson, of Gravesend, Long Island, had caught fifty-seven hundred shad "at one
hawl of a sein," and the next day sold "the greater
part of them in our markets."

Due to the glacial anomaly of the Hudson
River—a 160-mile fjord that commingled salt water,
freshwater, ice water, muddy water, and every other
conceivable mix—extant grocers' lists of seafood
for sale in eighteenth-century New York markets
could boast a miraculous variety, from blackfish to
weakfish, toadfish to dogfish, sheepshead, snook,
and porpoise. Faced with such astonishing plenty,
the citizens must have felt awe, they must have felt
fear, they must have felt pride, and they must have
felt a desire to taste it all.

In 1768 a forty-nine-foot whale appeared off

the coast of Coney Island, and unlike Moby-Dick, this one was caught and killed. Those were the days when the great Greenlander, the spermaceti, the humpback, razorback, finback, right whale, and grampus still swam the waters of New York. And whales were not the only giants that emerged from the deep. Five- and six-foot lobsters were common, and the scientific wonders never ceased: In 1834 the waters of Baltimore yielded a hundred-pound rockfish. In 1840 a three-foot oyster was hauled up in Alabama. In 1857 a stream in Paramus, New Jersey, yielded an eighteen-pound otter. In 1860 the Maine press publicized a striped bass that weighed 104 pounds. Thus it comes as no surprise that in 2006, when an angler named Mac Weakley pulled a record-setting twenty-five-pound largemouth bass from a reservoir outside San Diego, he threw it back. Presumably Weakley wanted to catch it again—when it grew bigger.

Nineteenth-century food publicity filled the press with outrageous accounts of primordial American foodstuffs: Out in the sticks there were caribou and antelope, epic beets the size of cedar stumps, and corn that grew so fast its percussion killed a hog. Even squash could grow to gigantic and powerful proportions, as one nineteenth-century New England farmer attested. "Why," he said,

> one of our squash vines chased a drove of hogs better'n half a mile, and they ran and squealed as if the old boy was after them.

Every nineteenth-century American, from savage frontiersman to effete Transcendentalist, could recite such mythology of American food.

The romance of westward expansion was a romance of the stomach, from superhuman ingestions to prodigious wastes. The recipe for cowboy sonofabitch stew included everything from beef brains to beef liver, tongue, heart, and bones. For America was a vast digestive force that understood the entire continent—if not the world—as its manifest dinner. Fabled eaters became fabled heroes, thunder-swallowing backwoodsmen like the Salt River Bully, buffalo-skin scarfers like Mike Fink, men who devoured alligators and rattlesnakes and blood and bragged of their "biler-iron bowels." Such an eater was Davy Crockett, who had a penchant for dining on bear bacon and bear steak. Now, bears are big. A single bear could make for weeks and weeks of meals. One year Crockett slaughtered more than one hundred such beasts.

Beyond eating bear, Crockett, as legend has it, scalped Indians with his teeth (and not the kind of Indian that grew on cobs). After one particularly gruesome massacre, he shared the tattered flesh of his vanquished foes with his dog. And as Crockett's political ambitions grew, Crockett folklore accelerated the embrace of violence and eating:

> I'm that same David Crockett, fresh from the
> backwoods, half horse, half alligator, a little
> touched with snapping turtle, can wade the

Mississippi, leap the Ohio, ride a streak of
lightning, slip without a scratch down a
honey locust. I can whip my weight in wild
cats, hug a bear too close for comfort, and
eat any man opposed to Jackson.

So Crockett, the congressman from the cane-
brakes, was a cannibal for the cause of Andrew Jackson. No surprise: Discovered by Columbus as a
particularly unsavory feature of the New World, the
inalienable right to conquer the other by devouring
him had made Europe shudder and shadowed the
conquistadors, the first settlers, and all who came
after. For Davy Crockett's blood-soaked esophagus
was no isolated monument in American history.
Early food media—in particular, the popular newspapers known as penny dreadfuls—often featured the
horrors of cannibalism at sea. In 1820 a supersized
cetacean staved in a ship called the *Essex*, the crew re-
paired to lifeboats, and when two of them died, they
furnished nourishment for the survivors. Even
Moby-Dick had Queequeg, its resident cannibal. For
Melville understood American yearnings, our hunger for blank doom, our propensity, as he wrote,

to bolt down all events, all creeds, and beliefs, and persuasions, all things visible and
invisible, never mind how knobby.

Thus the sad tale of Liver-Eating Johnson, who
hunted down and consumed Crow Indians to avenge

the murder of his wife. Thus did Colorado's
Slumgullion Pass became the original "Dead Man's
Gulch," the spot where a gold prospector named
Alferd Packer murdered and consumed five of his
fellow fortune hunters. The cannibal from Colorado
went to prison in 1874, only to resurface eighteen
years later as a tabloid celebrity, the hero of ballads,
and an enduring source of fascination among the
Court TV and *Forensic Files* crowd. Today, at the
University of Colorado at Boulder, you can sit down
to a meal at the Alferd Packer Grill.

Not only did westward expansion present an-
thropophagy as an unsavory yet practical energy bar
for desperate parties of lost miners and wagoners,
cannibalism also emerged as a way for the middling
frontiersman to make a name for himself. As he
drove his Conestoga ever deeper into the great
nowhere, the aspiring American legend eventually
came to understand that taboo nourishment presented an opportunity to become more legendary
than ever before: "I'm a slayer and a slaughterer,"
cried the otherwise not particularly noteworthy
backwoodsman from Wolfville. "An' I cooks an'
eats my dead!"

"I'm the man they call Sudden Death and General Desolation!" roared Mark Twain's Mississippi
raftsman.

I take nineteen alligators and a bar'l of
whiskey for breakfast when I'm in robust

health, and a bushel of rattlesnakes and a dead body when I'm ailing. . . . Blood's my natural drink.

If the dinner hour approached and a living person could not be found, the next best thing was meat. Raw meat. Even the pacifist Henry David Thoreau was not immune to such excitements. One pleasant evening at Walden Pond he spotted a wild wood-chuck and felt an overwhelming urge to devour the animal alive.

About a decade before Walden, Catharine Beecher had declared that

a person who lives chiefly on animal food is under a higher degree of stimulus than if his food was chiefly composed of vegetable substances.

As today, the implications of meat eating drove to the heart of American moral, political, medical, and aesthetic life: "If the stomach is fed with sour bread and burnt meats," warned the Beecher sisters in 1869, "it will raise such rebellions that the eyes will see no beauty anywhere." In 1902 Sarah Tyson Rorer summed it up: "Men as a class eat too much meat."

The Picture of New York, an extremely dull tome written by a long-winded U.S. senator, Samuel Latham Mitchill, does have one merit: The book provides incontrovertible evidence that a nineteenth-century New Yorker struck with a galloping case of meat-eating mania could have ventured to the local market to purchase slaughtered raccoon ("inferior eating," judged the gourmand Thomas Farrington De Voe), groundhog ("the old ones are tolerably good"), porcupine ("very troublesome to skin after death"), skunk ("very sweet and savory"), and opossum ("tender, luscious, and well-flavored"). Markets in New York City, Cleveland, and throughout Iowa offered black-bear steaks and panther chops as late as 1823, and bison, elk, reindeer, and moose remained available far into the nineteenth century.

Like the rest of our intestinal obsessions, our much-hyped and much-deplored meat mania reaches back to the very beginning. When the Dutch first settled, New York City teemed with bears, buffalo, deer, wolves, foxes, beavers, otters, mink, and muskrat. The Indians ate them all, and the Europeans not only learned the trick but institutionalized the practice. In February of 1653 the Town of Manhattan formally became the City of New Amsterdam—and three years later the first governmental meat regulations took effect. Every butcher had to take a solemn oath of office, and an official "slaughter certificate" had to confirm that any animal brought to market had been killed by consent of its owner. In 1657 the first "inspector of salted meats," a man by the name of Hendricks, was appointed.

Forty years after the first Dutch meat market had been established, the New Amsterdam Court, aware that the space originally designated for buying and selling roasts and steaks had become woefully inadequate for the thriving trade, designated a much grander space near the East River for what would soon become known as the "Great Flesh Market." (It was in this general vicinity that, until quite recently, New York's Fulton Street Fish Market held sway.)

On July 23, 1788, a Great Federal Procession to honor the federal Constitution marched through Manhattan. Ten divisions swaggered in this parade, the second of which was made up entirely of butchers who carried a linen flag inscribed with the patriotic motto

Skin me well, dress me neat,
And send me aboard the federal fleet.

Behind the standard-bearers rumbled a float drawn by four horses, and on the float stood two more butchers and two apprentice boys who—to honor the nation's nascent Constitution—split lambs and sliced beef. One hundred horse-mounted butchers followed the float; then came the butchers' marching band. The parade reached its climax on a hill near Mulberry Street, at the foot of ten enormous tables loaded with all the fixings of a liberty feast, most notably a thousand-pound ox, roasted whole.

Eight years after the Great Federal Procession, Amelia Simmons's first indigenous cookbook was published in Hartford, and the first sentence consisted of a single word: "Beef." *American Cookery* began with the perennial American obsession, "How to choose Flesh," just as a few decades later, in the opening recipe of what would become the nineteenth century's most coveted cookbook, Miss Leslie began her instructions for "Family Soup" with the following meticulous advice:

> Take a shin or leg of beef that has been newly killed; the fore leg is best, as there is the most meat on it.

In 1821 an entrepreneur named Gibbons purchased twenty of the best cattle ever seen in New York City and ordered the animals butchered. For reasons that remain obscure, Gibbons felt compelled to hire carts to carry his meat through the streets. Some witnesses recall forty carts; others remember sixty. Either way, on March 13 about ten thousand pounds of beef promenaded from Sixty-first Street and the East River, down the principal avenues of New York City, accompanied by music, streamers, and American flags. The flies buzzed, the blood dripped over the mud and cobblestones, and the enraptured multitude stood mesmerized by the spectacle.

Thomas Farrington De Voe, unsung historian of the nineteenth century, was a butcher who became so obsessed with all the food Americans could consume that in 1867 he published *The Mar-*

ket Assistant, containing a brief description of every article of human food sold in the public markets of the cities of New York, Boston, Philadelphia, and Brooklyn. (He was, as New York's *Evening Express* proclaimed, a "prince among the butchers.") De Voe recounted the earliest promenades of beef, which he dubbed "fat parades," and commented that

> since that period, "fat beef" exhibitions have often taken place. Some of them were got up in the most imposing, as well as the most expensive manner.

De Voe described New York's Canal Celebration of 1825, which featured hundreds of mounted butchers in white aprons and check sleeves, a team of trumpeters, a float of living animals, another float heaped with their dead brothers and sisters, and a banner on which the butchers had emblazoned the following paradox:

We preserve by destroying.

In 1871 Buffalo Bill and General Philip Sheridan exploited our taste for the domination of unvarnished American nature by hosting massive prairie banquets, where elegant urbanites in black tie sat for hours under the open sky consuming dinners of

buffalo tail, salmi of prairie dog, roasted elk, antelope chops, and black-tailed deer.

> To dine with a glacier on a sunny day is a glo-
> rious thing and makes common feasts of
> meat and wine ridiculous,

wrote John Muir. But Buffalo Bill's dissolute gour-
mandism was a clear indication of the actual frontier's death. While the physical limits of American
expansion had been touched, the borders of eating
were nowhere in sight. And it was right about this
time of geographical stricture that American folklore introduced the greatest meat eater of all our
intestinal myth-men.

It must have come as some relief to the growing urban population that somewhere in the American wilderness roamed a giant named Paul Bunyan,
who would consume nothing but raw moose meat.
Bunyan lore relates that in order to feed his team
of forest-cleaving frontiersmen the lumberjack
arranged "six concrete mixers" around the hotcake
griddle,

> and a sixty-foot tank for each mixer for a
> reservoir, and traveling cranes to put the bat-
> ter in with . . .

When Paul Bunyan set up his logging camp in the
great forests of North Dakota, he employed three

hundred cooks to satiate his seven axmen. The tremendous cookhouse required three acres of timber every day to keep the fire stoked. Eating and logging, consuming food and consuming the earth, forest fires and the fires in men's stomachs—such brutal and gut-centric absorptions had become one and the same.

Thus began our enduring nostalgia for the good old days of gobbling whatever you could hunt down or dig up. The mythical Daniel Boone had been nourished (as one poetically inclined biographer put it)

> not upon the "wolf's milk"—but upon the abundance of mild and serene nature— upon the delicious esculence of her forest game, and fruits of her wild luxuriant vines.

And in typical fashion, Mark Twain took the same highfalutin idea and put it into the vernacular: "When I'm thirsty," roared his Mississippi River man, "I reach up and suck a cloud dry like a sponge."

Professional gurgitators walk in the shadows of such mythic heroes. But they know that the American stomach, through the grandiose horrors of its limitless expansion, can still become one with the earth, the sea, and the sky. "The stomach-sac," Walt Whitman proclaimed in his greatest poem. "Food, drink, pulse, digestion . . ."

O I *say these are not the parts and poems of the Body*
    only, but of the Soul,
O I *say now these are the Soul!*

"We celebrate Thanksgiving by eating the greatest number of plates," announced George Shea, chairman of the International Federation of Competitive Eating. "A nod to the Pilgrims' historic breaking of bread with the Indians."

But about halfway into the twelve-minute contest, something along the lines of a tryptophan catatonia began to overtake Dale Boone. "Mount Boone may erupt!" cried Shea, at which point Dale dropped face-first into the stuffing. The seething and gurgling Mount Boone (like American folklore's long-forgotten Colonel Nimrod Wildfire and the not-so-legendary Billy Earthquake) had become natural disaster incarnate, and it was not a pretty sight.

As Mount Boone collapsed, "Hungry" Charles Hardy (world records in cabbage and shrimp) and "Cookie" Jarvis (world records in ice cream, cannoli, Chinese dumplings, french fries, and grapes) rose to their feet for the purely metaphorical sprint to the finish.

At one minute remaining, however, it was clear that neither Jarvis nor Hardy would emerge victorious. It was Eric Booker who came through with a world-record 5½ pounds of Thanksgiving gone in 720 seconds. The cameras converged as George Shea presented the oversize, cranberry-sauce-smeared trophy, and behind the tables postgame interviews were in full swing. "I couldn't catch a burp," Jarvis explained to the assembled media.

"Damned string beans," mumbled Hardy.

After ten or fifteen minutes of postgame, the crowd began to thin, but talk among the eaters did not stray from their enduring obsession. The Carnegie Deli was right around the corner.

"You do the first sandwich," "Cookie" Jarvis told his fellows. "The second one's free."

"Sounds like a great deal," said Dale Boone, who had miraculously recovered from his meat sweats. "What are we doing after this?" The hero donned his coonskin hat and lumbered out to the wilds of Central Park South.

Gorging on Diets

It may be one of the truest maxims ever yet advanced by any of the gentlemen, has been that a distempered stomach is the origin of all diseases. But, sirs, whence is it that the Stomach is distempered?
—Cotton Mather, 1724

For a man to follow nature, to live according to physiological laws, or to obey God, is one and the same thing.
—Thomas L. Nichols,
Esoteric Anthropology, 1853

Nutrition, like religion, is extremely visceral.
—Barry Sears
Enter the Zone, 1995

The American stomach has long sought to dominate the world by devouring it, but the gut can impose its divine orders through subtler means. As I peered ever further down the national gullet, I realized that the stomach encompassed more than what it simply ingested. Yes, we are what we eat; but we are what we refuse to eat, too. And feasting and fasting were only the most extreme examples of our compulsive need to discipline, punish, idolatrize, and revere the intestinal tract. As for the American obsession with pure food and raw food, it no doubt springs from religious zeal, social idealism, and medical nostrum—but such desires could not have matured and flourished in a void. Here, dieting has long persisted as the stomach's high ground, its primary weapon in the struggle to reign over and above any other bodily organ—most notably, the mind. And one of the abiding particularities of this country is the extent to which our diet culture has depended on our diet books, the holy scriptures of the American stomach.

With such hoary struggles and dialectical conflicts in mind, I asked a friendly salesclerk at my local Borders bookstore for a printout of all his current diet books. About an hour later emerged twelve single-spaced pages, heralding, in small type, the existence of a collection of more than seven hundred titles. The clerk handed me the list and shook his head, perhaps wondering whether ever in the history of bookstore databases there had been such a textual purge.

Little did he know a steady emission of diet books has long afflicted American publishing, at least since the days when Emerson, Thoreau, and company were furiously scribbling curricular content for the next century's Am. Lit. courses. Those who shudder at the sight of Barry Sears's *Mastering the Zone* and Suzanne Somers's *Get Skinny on Fabulous Food* on bestseller lists should keep in mind that neither *Walden* nor *Moby-Dick* could boast sales anywhere near Sylvester Graham's edition of *Discourses on a Sober and Temperate Life* or Marx Edgeworth Lazarus's *Passional Hygiene and Natural Medicine: Embracing the Harmonies of Man with His Planet.*

"The science of gastrosophy," Lazarus wrote in 1852,

> will place epicurism in strict alliance with honor and the love of glory.
>
> Of all our enjoyments, eating being the first, the last, and the most frequent pleasure of man, it ought to be the principal agent of wisdom in the future harmony . . .
>
> A skillful gastrosophist, also expert in the functions of culture and medical hygiene, will be revered as an oracle of supreme wisdom.

And diet, Lazarus noted, "is the entire harmony of man with his planet and his universe . . . a theory of integral or social redemption."

A raft of scholars have expended their careers examining source material that may (or may not) account for the rise and fall of the Dutch in New

Amsterdam, the melodrama and folly of the Puritans in New England, the origins of the American Revolution, the remarkable development of the age of Jackson, and the singular bloom of American Transcendentalism. But who has paid proper attention to the far more popular and, arguably, more influential books about diet and digestion that wended their way throughout all those decades?

Millions of Americans decry the contradictory advice of today's diet books—high carb or high protein? vegan or paleo? cream or soy?—but no one seems to have noticed that virtually identical controversies have raged since our earliest days. And no one has bothered to wonder why.

> We have been nearly bored to death for the last fifteen years, with prosy moralities about health, and the dragchain of duty has been hitched on to the simplest offices of life, until what shall we eat, and what shall we drink, and wherewithal shall we be clothed, have come to be the all-absorbing meditations and discussions of a large class of cabbage-headed philosophers.

The "fifteen years" Marx Edgeworth Lazarus alludes to are 1837 to 1852. Then, as now, a marketplace glutted with too many choices had led to a plethora of taboos. As Catharine and Harriet Beecher noted soon after Dr. Lazarus,

Were one to believe all that is said and written on this subject, the conclusion probably would be that there is not one solitary article of food on God's earth which it is healthful to eat.

Indeed, the "Essay on Indigestion" was a standard issue nineteenth-century American essay, and for good reason: The *Encyclopedia Americana* of 1830 declared dyspepsia the most common of all American ailments. But the concerns of our most visionary nineteenth-century diet gurus transcended medicine, politics, economics, moral philosophy, and even losing weight. They believed that our relationship with food could forge a new relationship with nature, and thus satisfy the old American need to belong to the place where worms and skunks and the bark of trees had once been the primal diet. "If I were to use flesh in a way which I thought to be least injurious," wrote William Alcott,

I would select that of wild animals, apparently in full health and vigor, and of youthful or middle age, and use it with no condiments or accompaniments, except, perhaps, a small quantity of bread and salt, and with as little cooking of any kind as possible.

What was this but an aspiration to be like our first parents, to turn back time, to possess America as a true native and thus to be redeemed of our belatedness?

In 1796 Amelia Simmons published *American Cookery*, our country's first indigenous cookbook. Not only did Simmons provide explicit directions for decapitating turtles and cleaning their entrails, it was here, for the first time in English, that one could read descriptions of roast turkey garnished with "cramberry-sauce." Here appeared the first printed use of such odd words as "slapjack" and "shortning." Here the English-speaking world discovered a new dessert called a doughnut, made with pounds of either "superfine sugar," "double refined sugar," or the ubiquitous "cheap sugar." And the unapologetic Americanness of Simmons's cookbook could be discerned in her recipes for "Federal Pan Cake," "Independence Cake," and an "Election Cake" so capacious it called for thirty quarts of flour.

As the massive proportions of Simmons's baked goods indicate, our food mania reflects our titanic geography, our belief in social experimentation, our political idealism—in other words, the classic explanations offered up as excuses for American character and experience. Yet the outsize ambitions of the American stomach derive from less obvious sources, too; sources that have long been misunderstood, mislabeled, mischaracterized, and misread. In fact, the eighteenth-century development of our profound and peculiar relationship to diet books owes much to the guts of Benjamin Franklin. Few people have ever been more obsessed with the independent life of their stomach, from its judicious assimilations to its promiscuous projections.

Take this bizarre episode of his *Autobiography*, in which Franklin explained how and why he stopped being a vegetarian:

> I believe I have omitted mentioning that in my first voyage from Boston, being becalmed off Block Island, our people set about catching cod and hawl'd up a great many. Hitherto I had stuck to my resolution of not eating animal food . . . But I had formerly been a great lover of fish, and when this came hot out of the frying pan, it smelt admirably well. I balanced some time between principle and inclination: till I recollected, that when the fish were opened, I saw smaller fish taken out of their stomachs: —Then, thought I, if you eat one another, I don't see why we mayn't eat you. So I dined upon cod very heartily and continued to eat with other people, returning only now and then occasionally to a vegetable diet. So convenient a thing it is to be a reasonable creature, since it enables one to find or make a reason for every thing one has a mind to do.

Here, logical analysis has been twisted into the service of appetite. More than any other figure of his age, Franklin understood that the impulses of circulation and digestion would always trump rationality.

The heart of the second part of Franklin's *Autobiography* consists of the particulars of what he calls his "bold and arduous project of arriving at moral perfection." Franklin's "thirteen names of virtues" prescribe justice, duty, industry, sincerity, cleanliness, chastity, and humility—and even a casual reader cannot help but be reminded of his strongest literary antecedent, the Ten Commandments. Of course, the first commandment for the ancient Hebrew was, "Thou shalt have no other gods before me," whereas Franklin's first "virtue" is

TEMPERANCE.
Eat not to dullness,
drink not to elevation.

Now, the observant Jew must submit to numerous dietary laws, but none of these regulations dislocates Yahweh from his preeminent place in the hierarchy of belief. By placing diet above every other "commandment" given to his new nation, Benjamin Franklin laid bare his fear (founded in his own belly) that any and all unreasonable urges to consume must be disciplined.

Of course, when it came to food, Franklin painted himself as the quintessence of moderation. He went so far as to insist that

little or no notice was ever taken of what related to the victuals on the table, whether it
was well or ill drest, in or out of season, of
good or bad flavour, preferable or inferior to
this or that other thing of the kind; so that I
was bro't up in such a perfect inattention to
those matters as to be quite indifferent what
kind of food was set before me; and so un-
observant of it, that to this day, if I am ask'd
I can scarce tell, a few hours after dinner,
what I din'd upon.

It is safe to say that potbellied Ben was in denial.
How else to explain Franklin's disavowal of food in
the face of not one but two hyperbolic essays he
wrote about Indian? The flavor of corn, rhapsodized
Franklin,

is one of the most agreeable and whole-
some ... in the world; that its green ears
roasted are a delicacy beyond expression; that
samp, hominy, succatash, and nokehock,
made of it, are so many pleasing varieties;
and that a johny, or a hoe-cake, hot from the
fire, is better than a Yorkshire muffin.

(Nokehock was parched corn cooked in hot ashes,
then pounded into meal; samp, a porridge made
from beaten or boiled corn, eaten hot or cold with
milk or butter.) In fact, Benjamin Franklin was so
obsessed with what he ate that he had his own diet

guru, a British mystic who endowed food and digestion with extraordinary, universal powers.

Franklin's "master," Thomas Tryon, had founded his own Hindu-inspired vegetarian society in London, from which he declared sugar morally suspect and promulgated a religion that called for the adoption of a "clean" diet (not to be confused with the Clean Out Herbal Diet System®, propounded by Dr. Alan Frisher in 1989). "Let your food be simple, and drinks innocent," Tryon wrote in the first vegetarian cookbook, *A Bill of Fare of Seventy-Five Noble Dishes.* With only a smattering of competition west of Iran, Thomas Tryon soon became the seventeenth century's most famous vegetarian.

Tryon's magnum opus, *The Way to Health*, bulges with learned treatises on "Fatness," "Food Proper for Children," and "The Mischief of Variety of Meats," along with chapters devoted to "The Cause of Wars" (food related), "How to Cure Wounds" (use food), and "The Reasons in Nature Why Cities and Great Towns are Subject to the Pestilence" (it has something to do with the food). At its most visionary moments, *The Way to Health* unfolds its own epistemology and ontology, not to mention a metaphysics of space:

> The root of all knowledge that man is capable of, is in himself: Therefore if any will understand any thing truly, he must first turn the eye of his mind inward, not outward.

But how could a phenomenon born in the outward realm—a piece of celery, for example—contribute in any way whatsoever to the root of all knowledge, when according to Tryon's mystical revelation the truth can only originate from within? Thomas Tryon solved the problem very simply, by granting food its own inward spirit, a "digestive faculty" that elucidated its "true virtue." (And Tryon's argument has stayed with us. Raw food and vegan blogs and Web sites continue to argue the case that food possesses its "spiritous parts, and if any violence be done to them in the preparation, then such food becomes dull and half dead.")

According to Master Tryon, if we can restrict our diet to those foods and preparations that most thoroughly contain "spiritous parts," we may enhance our "true judgment":

> ... for the spirits of men are not earthly things, to receive their nourishment through the organs by the concoction of meats and drinks only, but derive their purer aliment like spunges through the whole body, from the clear thin vapours of the air, which do powerfully penetrate the body on all sides, but are hindered through superfluity of meats and drinks; and so the spirits in the body, for want of being found with these refreshing gales, become thick, and as it were suffocated.

It may come as no surprise that Tryon asserted that "oatmeal is to be accounted the best of all flour, by reason of its preparation, the body of the grain being open'd and the inward spirit as it were set at liberty." Young Ben Franklin could be forgiven for his insistence that "a large porringer of hot water-gruel" for breakfast would bring us all one step closer to utopia. To Franklin, eating oatmeal (the "inward spirit" of which had been "set at liberty") may have quite logically seemed to be nothing less than a rehearsal for the birth of American independence—in his own ample gut.

Franklin's worship of balanced digestive circulations went so far as to apply Tryon's strange theories to something as simple and basic as getting a good night's sleep. In "The Art of Procuring Pleasant Dreams," Franklin ridiculed prevailing attitudes of aerophobia by recommending a steady supply of fresh air in the bedroom, and advocated "thinner and more porous bed-clothes, which will suffer the perspirable matter more easily to pass through them."

And then there is the issue of money. Generations of narrow-minded critics have dismissed Franklin because of his profane preoccupation, expressed in his dicta that a fat kitchen maketh a lean will, and that nothing but money is sweeter than honey. None of these detractors has considered the possibility that when Franklin spoke of money he was merely articulating the visceral desires of the brain in his gut.

Take the first metaphor of Franklin's "The Way

to Wealth," an essay whose title perhaps not so co-incidentally mirrors Thomas Tryon's *The Way to Health*. Here, Franklin likens money to "solid Pudding"—and this marriage of custard and cash is no coincidence. Throughout the 1750s, Franklin had argued for an increase in Philadelphia's paper currency. According to Franklin, a lack of "a sufficient medium" to conduct trade required an "emission" of credit. Thus did Franklin seek to increase the state's economic power much in the same way as a healthy stomach would process the spiritous parts of food into bodily powers, while getting rid of the dross. As always, strong emissions implied healthy circulations.

For Franklin, the individual body had become one large system of assimilation and dispersion, a great sponge of absorbent mouths—from lungs to pores to eyeballs—that must carefully choose what and what not to imbibe. And on July 4, 1776, Franklin's revolutionary peers pronounced their body politic commensurate to the body digestive, just as determined to dissolve all relationship with unhealthy foreign bodies.

Despite Dr. Franklin's essay in its defense, even the most innocent hasty pudding would eventually join the hosts of other fateful American eating taboos. Just as red meat and carbohydrates have both run the gamut from Savior to Satan in our national consciousness, so corn mush, "the purest of all food," the manna that had graced Puritan tables as early as that first Thanksgiving, would eventually discover detractors among America's gastrosophical elite.

> I never knew a child who was indulged largely and frequently in hasty pudding and milk, or hasty pudding and molasses, who had not a sour stomach, or worms in the intestines, or both,

Dr. William Andrus Alcott warned in 1838.

> Few things are more deceptive to children or adults, than these soft lazy dishes.

Dr. Alcott's declaration of war on hasty pudding (the trans fat of its time) typified the stark disagreements that festered among nineteenth-century American food experts: Were potatoes good or evil? Should food be eaten by itself or mixed with other ingredients? Should anything ever be mashed?

Only eight years before Alcott's attack on hasty pudding, Lydia Maria Child, in her bestselling cookbook, had declared the opposite to be the case:

> If the system is in a restricted state, nothing can be better than rye hasty pudding and West India molasses. This diet would save many a one the horrors of dyspepsia.

Like Benjamin Rush and John Harvey Kellogg, Lydia Maria Child devoted a great deal of her intellectual genius to digestion. And while she possessed a keen grasp of suet, lard, slops, vinegars, and sour beer, she had also studied Milton, Scott, Gibbon, Addison, and Shakespeare, and ran in the same social circle as the greatest thinkers of her day, including Ralph Waldo Emerson and John Greenleaf Whittier. Along with her cookbooks, Child wrote novels and antislavery polemics, women's education tracts, histories, biographies, and songs ("Over the river and through the woods/to Grandmother's house we go!"). Perhaps most influential of all, she wrote *The American Frugal Housewife: Dedicated to Those Who Are Not Ashamed of Economy.*

The abolitionist William Lloyd Garrison compared Child's gastrosophical revelations to the almanacs of Benjamin Franklin, "for they embody his wisdom, his sagacity, and his wonderful knowledge of human nature." And like Franklin's work, *The American Frugal Housewife* had not targeted the elite. Lydia Child was of the people, and her first rule was simple:

Look frequently to the pails to see that nothing is thrown to the pigs which should have been in the grease-pot.

Just as the Food Network's Emeril Lagasse brought hockey fans to food television and made the cable channel the "Emeril Network," Lydia Maria Child broadened the diet-book audience, and by doing so became an international star. She was like a cross between Susan Sontag and Suzanne Somers, an intellectual and a writer who was a celebrity, a hostess, a diet-book writer, and a cultural critic. Child also belonged in the spiritual company of Cotton Mather and Thomas Tryon—in *The American Frugal Housewife*, food could answer any problem, mental or physical. It was of use not only to eat, but to glue things together (rye paste); to clean your hands and to wash silk (boiled potatoes); to cure dysentery, croup, colic, jaundice, and piles; and (in the case of skim milk) to paint bricks. "New England rum," she mused, "constantly used to wash the hair, keeps it very clean."

Like so many explorers and investigators who came before and after, Child brought science to bear on the stomach. She advocated ointments made of plantains and leeks boiled in cream, she warned of the unhealthy influence of cucumbers, and she soberly noted "there is more deception in geese than in any other kind of poultry." Which is not to say Child did not offer plenty of hard-core cooking instruction. When preparing calf's head, Child advised, it is better to leave the windpipe on. If it hangs out of the pot while the head is cooking, all the froth will escape through it. As for roasting pork, when the eyes drop out, the pig is half done.

Above all, Child advocated one of the first and

last of all American maxims: Eat simple food. And one other thing:

> Avoid the necessity of a physician, if you can, by careful attention to your diet.

The most famous graduate of Yale Medical School's class of 1827, William Andrus Alcott advocated birth control, education reform, and is generally credited with the earth-shattering invention of the student desk with individual shelves and a hinged blackboard. But it was food reform, and particularly his advocacy of a pure and perfect appetite, that he hoped would hasten the restoration of fallen humanity. It was an outsize aspiration but typical of the perfectionist visions that marked the heyday of American stomach science. For diet reform did not only mean health. As the increasingly frenetic development of Jacksonian America enabled some families to eat turtle soup while others had to content themselves with pigeon, diet reform meant the possibility for economic justice: By following Alcott's advice, struggling young mothers could spend less time in the kitchen and more time educating their progeny.

In time-honored tradition, William Alcott attempted to convince the multitude of the necessity for food reform by painting an anxiety-ridden picture of the helpless American child:

Have the quantity, quality and condition of
the food and the drink which are introduced
to a child's stomach, and which, when assim-
ilated, course their way through every part
of the living machine twenty-five or thirty
thousand times every twenty-four hours,
nothing to do with character?

The simple fact of having a kid under her care
meant that the American housewife was "treading at
every moment on the verge of destruction, physical
and moral." And since her drooling tot, like everything else American, must reach "the perfection of
its nature," Mama must not create appetites "perverted by exciting food and drink":

Confectionary, and bad food, and bad
drinks, and uncontrolled passions, and mis-
placed affections . . . are the prolific source
of half the licentiousness with which our
earth is afflicted, and changed from an
Eden to a scene of mourning, lamentation
and woe.

Shakes and fries bad, fresh vegetables good. As
for wheat mush and rye mush, raw milk, gruel, and
whortleberries—according to William Alcott these
were redemptive and Adamic aliments. In order to
attain intellectual, moral, nervous, and social dis-
tinction, citizens must subsist on rice, barley, oats,

potatoes, beans, peas, millet, beets, carrots, parsnips, turnips, onions, radishes, squash, pumpkins, gourds, cabbages, lettuce, tomatoes, celery, Indian—and not much else.

Throughout his long career, William Alcott sought "truly philosophic viands," food from which he was able to discern sublime truths. "Nothing ought to be mashed before it is eaten," he declared. "This is a universal rule—almost as much so as that two and two make four." According to Alcott, the science of the time had proven that "flesh and fish, and high seasoned food" caused terrible excitement in the "nerves of the stomach, and through them on the brain and nervous system generally." With immense political implications: The enervation that inevitably followed the rush of nervous excitement produced by the depraved eating of overstimulating animal flesh not only gives you gas but "sinks rapidly the nation." At this point American food paranoia reached an apex. It was digestion that could save us, or send us to hell.

Henry David Thoreau, the self-proclaimed nonconformist hermit, had as a young man lamented how much of his well-being depended "on the condition of my lungs and stomach." At Walden Pond he had seen spring's fluorescence as a purgation of "excrements of all kinds." And years later, at the conclusion of his essay "Life Without Principle," Thoreau laid out his American dream—that human society and our daily routine, that politics and spirituality and consciousness itself, should emulate involuntary digestive processes.

> Not only individuals, but States, have thus a confirmed dyspepsia, which expresses itself, you can imagine by what sort of eloquence. . . . Why should we not meet, not always as dyspeptics, to tell our bad dreams, but sometimes as eupeptics, to congratulate each other on the ever glorious morning?

Thoreau's epiphany would have gone nowhere in any country but America, where Benjamin Franklin had conflated oatmeal and liberty, where Marx Edgeworth Lazarus had dubbed the gut

> the central organ and sovereign of life, at once the seat of physical and of spiritual reception . . . ,

and where yet another nineteenth-century American gastrosophist, James Wilkinson (author of *The Human Body and Its Connection with Man*), could consider each human being a "universal eater."

Like the Puritans before them, the men and women of the 1850s believed that specially graced eating practices went hand in hand with social and spiritual separatism. The most extreme of the diet gurus convinced their followers to turn their backs on digestive depravity and form their own sects. William Alcott's transcendentalist cousin Bronson founded a community called Fruitlands. In a farmhouse in central Massachusetts, he ordained a diet of fruit and whole-grain bread (the wheat must be grown without manure), a diet he declared the only path to eternal salvation. No alcohol, caffeine, warm water, or sex; no bought goods, no private property, no fish, milk, eggs, butter, or cheese. Rumor had it Alcott's acolytes disparaged the potato for growing downward, and thus failing to aspire. The social experiment lasted only from the summer to the winter of 1843, six months of peristaltic perfection. Bronson's daughter and William Alcott's first cousin once removed, Louisa May Alcott, loathed every minute.

Longer lived than Fruitlands has been Seventh-Day Adventism, the dietary version of Christianity founded by America's "Prophetess of Health," Ellen Harmon White. (Her most famous disciple was Dr. John Harvey Kellogg.) "Flesh was never the best food," wrote Prophetess White.

> Its use is now doubly objectionable, since disease in animals is so rapidly increasing.

Clearly White's religious revelations must have included a vision of mad cow.

Seventh-Day Adventism's nineteenth-century restrictions have blossomed into a denomination of thirteen million, and the sect's lacto-ovo-vegetarian Web site urges whole grains, fruit, and at least ten glasses of water a day. A devotee must avoid consumption of fried food, margarine, alcohol, stimulants, and television. Such limitations demonstrate faith in Christ, an equation of diet and dogma that connects American religious groups as far afield as seventeenth-century separatists and late twentieth-century Christian UFO cults. Even the suicidal Heaven's Gate congregation professed religious reasons for alimentary denial: The extraterrestrials (who supposedly touched down right around the time of the Last Supper) possessed atrophied digestive systems.

At Fruitlands the Alcott family had been joined by a crew that included Samuel Larned, whose dietary fanaticism had already impelled him to spend one year of his life eating nothing but crackers; another year he had subsisted entirely on apples. Such single-substance diets were not all that unusual in America. They emerged naturally from our reaction to abundance and our rage for dietetic order. Cotton Mather himself had observed that "a milk-diet is exceeding friendly to the nerves," that a diet of whey and nothing but whey could cure rheumatism, and that kidney stones could be cured by "The Turtle-Diet." In 1751 John Wesley advised those who suffered from scurvy to "live on turnips for a month."

An offhand note by William Alcott indicates that by the middle of the nineteenth century, single-substance had become something of a movement:

> They who think we should confine our-
> selves, through life, chiefly to one article of
> food, or even to a very few, should not select
> the peach.

(Alcott based his suspicion of the fruit on its
"stringy nature.") In fact, William Alcott became
America's first champion of the principle that
everything should be eaten by itself. "Whenever the
plum is eaten," he declared, "it should be eaten
alone." Furthermore, "rice, whether baked or
boiled, is best eaten alone." As for beans and peas
and meat and fish and corn:

> The perfection of their use consists in mak-
> ing one entire meal—perhaps two—each
> day, of a single article . . . without any addi-
> tion of condiments, sauces, or gravies.

And so the worship of "pure, plain, unperverted
pudding." Thus the fear that a mince pie (which
might actually consist of eighteen or twenty different ingredients) would "stupify our immortal
souls."

Bizarre as they may seem, Alcott's theories at-
tracted followers and became the basis for a popular
movement. As the antebellum world became more
and more complex and dangerous, the food isolationism of single-substance eating not only provided
a satisfying sense of simplicity, but an emblem of political isolationism. At a time when the complications

of economics, politics, and morals threatened to engulf all in violence, single-substance consumption highlighted our hopes for a self-sufficient, separate peace.

The turn of this latest century has produced yet another glut of diet experts hell-bent on convincing us that the transformations of our bodies will revolutionize consciousness itself, and vice versa. Like the great Puritan divine Jonathan Edwards, these modern intestinal preachers are still railing against sinners in the hands of an angry stomach, "stuck in carbohydrate hell," and declaring that "when patients lose excess body fat, it's as if the hand of God touched them." To these exhortations, Dr. Barry Sears (author of *Enter the Zone*) adds that the stories he retells "are not unlike the typical testimonials that you'd expect to hear at a faith-healing revival meeting." The late Dr. Robert Atkins (*Dr. Atkins' Diet Revolution*) identified himself as "an evangelist." And Victoria Moran (*Love Yourself Thin*) vows that the first sacred "affirmation" must be, "I eat in love, not in guilt." Among today's glut of Christian, South Beach, New Age, paleo, calorie-restriction, and other assorted denominations of diet dogmas, Marx Edgeworth Lazarus's 150-year-old warning remains current: If the American stomach refuses to heed medical and spiritual demands, if it refuses to discriminate among the great plenty at its disposal, it will surely "be caught in the gastric or abdominal department of the hells."

Because they are all sects of the one true American religion, each of the modern American diets arrives packaged with its own creation myth. Barry Sears's eicosanoids (the prime movers of his Zone Diet) "have been around for more than five hundred million years," while Dr. Atkins insisted that his D-Zerta, Baken-Ets, and pork-rind regimen is most closely aligned with the primal diet:

> As cavemen, we humans evolved mainly on a diet of meat. And that's what our bodies were and are built to handle. For fifty million years our bodies had to deal with only minute amounts of carbohydrates. . . .

Meanwhile, Robert Pritikin profoundly intoned,

> Let me take you back through the long tunnel of time to a point in human evolution when the modern humans, the first Adam and Eve, were born into the original garden. . . .

Pritikin subsequently backed his claim that our collective grandparents were eating grilled vegetables from that "original garden" by minute analyses of coprolite, the petrified feces of early humans. In *The Pritikin Weight Loss Breakthrough*, he unveiled the carnal "couch potato . . . in our genes." Such inherited biological drives are, like any satanic emanation worth its salt, temptations that must be vanquished. And so Pritikin announced that

> we can no longer live by instinct alone.
> Patterns of behavior that long ago were unconscious, and imposed upon us by the environment, must now be practiced consciously
> if we are to achieve optimal health.

We do not diet. By denying our instincts, we raise our consciousness. Which roughly translates into the following koan: I want tepid gruel for breakfast, lunch, and dinner; ergo, this is not a diet. (Repeat one hundred times.)

Peter J. D'Adamo, who bases his dietary theories on blood type, plumbs the depths of our antiquated guts even more deeply than Pritikin's disinterment of ancient shitting grounds. D'Adamo proclaims that the science of "paleoserology" has shown that

> blood types are as fundamental as creation
> itself. . . . They are the signature of our ancient ancestors on the indestructible parchment of history.

Way back in 1840 Miss Leslie offered a recipe for "Eve's Pudding." No surprise that today Kabbalah has become an energy drink ("a delicious citrus fusion") and men like Jordan Rubin, author of *The Maker's Diet*, can assert that in order to be thin, fit, and healthy, simply eat what Jesus ate. And just in case you can't find organic hyssop at the local ShopRite, Rubin's own Garden of Life company offers pills of goat's milk whey blended with a biblically certified mélange of amylase, lipase, alpha-galactosidase, and cellulase. In June 2004 *Entrepreneur* magazine hailed Garden of Life as the fifth-fastest-growing business in America.

Of course, gut-centric medical theories have long reigned in this country, from the pukes of Cotton Mather to the venesections of Benjamin Rush and all the way up to Atkins, who proposed that the way we eat is to blame not only for how overweight Americans are but for a host of disorders familiar to readers of pharmaceutical side-effect warnings:

> Irritability, nervousness, dizziness, headaches, faintness, cold sweats, cold hands and feet, weak spells, drowsiness, forgetfulness, insomnia, worrying, confusion, anxiety, palpitations of the heart, muscle pains, hostility, belligerence, antisocial behavior, indecisiveness, crying spells, lack of concentration, twitching of muscles, gasping for breath.

From the Puritans to the Federalists to the gastrosophists and beyond, mental health has depended upon gastric health. Every ailment stems from improper aliment.

While one group of our present-day crop of food prophets looks to ancient history and the spiritual qualities of diet (in the tradition of Thomas Tryon and William Alcott), another transforms the quest into a cutting-edge scientific program. Dr. Neal Barnard, a faculty member at the medical school of George Washington University, recently asserted in an interview with the *Los Angeles Times* that

> cheese is like a drug. It has the same addictive qualities as sugar, chocolate or meat.

Barnard's book *Breaking the Food Seduction* declares that the digestion of cheese releases "a whole host of opiates." Just as the recovering heroin addict must reprogram his mind, the recovering cheese addict must reprogram his intestines. Thus has Hugo Liu from the MIT media lab compiled a recipe database not of ingredients but of 100,000 distinct emotions. (The *New York Times* reported that prospective users of said database may not only search for ecstatic cheese, but for "sad" oatmeal, "poetic" pizza, or "pensive" deviled eggs.) And just in case the ventral software malfunctions, Barry Sears's *Enter the Zone* provides "Technical Support," a toll-free tech-help number.

The practice of scientific eating reached an apex of sorts in the early twentieth century, with the ascendancy of measurement-obsessed diet gurus such as Fannie Farmer, MIT-educated Ellen Richards (author of *The Chemistry of Cooking and Cleaning* and

The Dietary Computer), and Professor W. O. Atwater of Wesleyan University, who in the spring of 1896 created a stir in the penny press when he locked a student named Smith into an airtight chamber bursting with thermometers, hygrometers, condensers, pumps, and fans. Atwater sedulously recorded Smith's food intake (which included baked beans, "Hamburg steak," and mashed potatoes) and the amount of energy Smith expended lifting weights and studying physics, and after innumerable calculations the professor emerged with a unit of food measurement he called the calorie.

Of course, what Cotton Mather had called "Cook-pedantry" ("eating and drinking exactly by weight and measure") had been as widespread in the seventeenth as in the twentieth century. But Sarah Tyson Rorer's "scientific cookery" reached new heights by comparing "the living machine, the human body, to the railroad engine or locomotive." Rorer's *New Cook Book* of 1902 featured such must-read chapters as "A Few Edible Weeds" and "Vegetables Containing Nitrogenous Matter without Starch or Sugar."

Benjamin Franklin had been the first to merge American diet culture, science culture, and capitalism. Today the ultimate maximize-your-personal-profit high-tech diet can be found in the capitalized, trade-marked, exclamation-pointed *SUGAR BUSTERS!*™ In this *New York Times* bestseller, H. Leighton Steward (a Fortune 500 CEO) and a team of doctors expressed dietary perfection to be the gospel of corporate America. As CEOs of our bodies, we can regulate our metabolism as a capitalist exercise. Like money within the economic system, food within the digestive tract follows iron laws of consolidation and dispersal as "units" that may or may not move into or out of the system at optimal "rates." Blood-cholesterol levels become a matter of the "manufacture" and "distribut[ion]" of glucose, while fat and excess calories can be completely excised through a "constant restructuring" of corporate gullet. We're not dieting, we're exercising our God-given American right to maximize profitability.

From the esoteric and spiritual Tryon/Alcott end of the spectrum has emerged the likes of Victoria Moran and her *Love Yourself Thin: The Revolutionary Spiritual Approach to Weight Loss*. This is not a book that proposes molecular layoffs so much as a "love-powered release of weight." Only "love can revolutionize your relationship with food"; only love can regulate "your love-powered cholesterol level."

Whereas the late Dr. Robert Atkins prescribed megadoses of vitamins to make up for all those vegetables you're not eating, Moran insists that "the most important nutritional element is vitamin YOU," which can only be "activated by contact with a Higher Power." In the killer corporate world of *SUGAR BUSTERS!™*, we feast on antelope and alligator. *Love Yourself Thin* is strictly vegan. "Spirituality is the inner side; gentle, natural food choices the outer."

But after a while Victoria Moran and the spiritual diet crew begin to sound less like Puritans and more like a hokey rip-off of the sublime harmonic convergences of American Transcendentalism. Based on what you choose to put in your stomach, "you can establish your own unique connection with universal love." And so on and so forth. We have heard it all before. Moran's dietary koans firmly align her with the post-Puritan heritage of self-reliance—our perfect, Emersonian faith in involuntary perception, the sleepless brain in the gut.

But Moran's philosophical borrowings pale before the vast appropriations of the greatest synthesizer of American diet history, who has at long last descended from the clouds. The most compelling indication that "the future harmony" is upon us must be the presence of Suzanne Somers, the bona fide prophetess, our luminous spirit in the flesh. As Walt Whitman advised long ago, Somers contains multitudes: Her dietary Vegas act parades everybody's routines. She lip syncs Barry Sears's technical language of insulin secretions into the bloodstream and sashays his assertion that "cholesterol and fat are essential to health." In the great tradition of William Alcott and the Beecher sisters, she abhors "white flour" and asserts a doctrine of "control" over diet. Like Atkins, she blabs that "I eat whenever I am hungry. . . . I eat until I am full, and I never skip meals." She swallows whole and then regurgitates Steward's doctrine: "Sugar is the body's greatest enemy!" Like Victoria Moran, she declares herself "a recovering sugar addict" and knowingly adds that we eat "to fill some emotional void." Like D'Adamo, she gushes that when her "cells thrive," she can "feel empowered."

Somers's transcendental zone of the perfect stomach is a misty never-never land of personal, economic, and domestic bliss meticulously documented on every overproduced page of her modern gastrosophical masterpiece, *Get Skinny on Fabulous Food* (which reached number one on the *New York Times* list). Every square pica of the book has been peppered with casual snapshots of Somers posing with beautiful stuffed zucchini flowers or her darling granddaughter Daisy. "I can't give my home phone number to everyone," she laments, and we almost believe her.

Get Skinny on Fabulous Food is nothing less than the voice heard in our eternally howling gastric wilderness, and Somers's glistening body, the redemptive core of all enteric effluvia. Even without that phone number, we can achieve intimacy through the act of "Somersizing," by which we become one with her perfect flesh. And there are dividends to digestive election: Once Somersizing has been achieved, "any questions you have will be answered by your own body."

And there you have it.

Perhaps it's the beginning of something new, perhaps the final stroke. Either way, the history of the American diet book has led straight back to your own, infallible flesh. Any questions?

A long time ago only Yahweh knew the answers, and beneath his implacable gaze our muscle and fat became ashes and dust. In order to teach the Chosen how to stay that way, Moses divided the milk from the meat and proclaimed the pig and eel unclean. A few thousand years after that, Mather and Franklin and Alcott and Child and Atkins and Sears and Somers declared that the answer to any question, great or small, could be reduced to what you would or would not put into your own divine stomach. Today there exists no question too arcane or abstruse for the gut. Except, perhaps, for this: If the diet gospel is to remain a matter of holy inspiration, who writes that final chapter?

The one about the apocalypse.

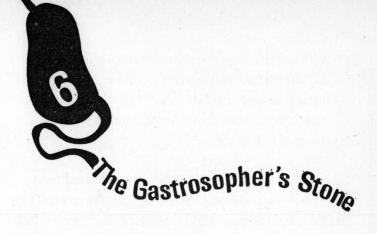

The Gastrosopher's Stone

Of Man's first disobedience, and the fruit
Of that forbidden tree, whose mortal taste
Brought death into the world, and all our woe . . .
—John Milton, 1667

It all started on the slippery slope of looking at alterna-
tive species. As soon as one was found, my philosophical
question for the whole situation was what do they expect
us to do? Write a paper? But now we're embroiled in the
whole—"should we allow this thing in?"
—Standish K. Allen, 2005

Thomas Farrington De Voe, the great nineteenth-century chronicler of butchered meats and store-bought fruits and vegetables, recorded that a famished American would not have to travel far before encountering a ready-made feast of wild-growing

chestnuts, beechnuts, walnuts, butternuts, hazelnuts, mulberries, cherries, currants, plums, gooseberries, medlars, bilberries, blackberries, raspberries, cranberries, and strawberries; the latter in such abundance, that people lay down in the fields and ate them to satiety.

Supine, his stomach bulging with masticated fruit—here lies an enduring image of the American ingester, an eater who would not stop until every last berry was gone.

And gone they are.

High-tech hybrids dominate today's $1.4 billion strawberry industry, which almost exclusively produces, distributes, and purveys FX ananassa, the bright-red, firm-skinned, ever-in-season, disease-resistant, bulbous, pulpy, and tasteless supermarket species. We're talking cultivation-friendly fruit, the fruit that doesn't bruise when it ships, the fruit that looks irresistible under the lights of Bernie Gelson, Stew Leonard, and King Kullen. Fruit like the Heritage raspberry, a variety that Cornell University invented and released in 1969, which has since become the most widely grown red raspberry in the world.

Our brave new fruit must possess the proper sweetness, the proper machine harvestability, the proper curvature, the proper mist-moistened glisten, and the proper aroma profile. Raspberry DNA will eventually be twisted and woven into the perfect cultivar, a thornless plant that stands upright and barks when it is thirsty. And that single, sublime

raspberry genotype will live long and prosper—
while all that old, antiquated raspberry rubbish will
languish and die. No matter that commercial raspberries date back to 1737, when they were sold from
America's first nursery; no matter that the genetic
base of the ancient fruit will narrow to a single
thread, one virus away from extinction. Hell, we
bred the goddamned variety, gave it life in the first
place. Now the fruit wants immortality?

Recent news reports have declared that within a
decade, the banana may become extinct. If it does, it
will have been destroyed by its perfection. In the
1880s Americans hardly knew bananas existed.
Then from Boston, home of the Pilgrims, emerged
the United Fruit Company (now known as Chi-
quita), which exploited and monopolized and
railroaded and easemented the way to mass consumption of its product. By the 1930s bananas
drooped from supermarket shelves, and a generation of Ellis Island immigrants could recall a yellow
fruit as their first American meal. These days 55 million tons of bananas bulldoze their way into the
market every year, a number dominated by a single
variety, a chromosome-addled Cavendish dwarf
commonly known as the dessert banana. Cassan-
dras of the Cavendish prophesy that the inbred and
cloned fruit will one day be walloped by disease, and
the world's banana population exterminated. Even
those who pooh-pooh the threat of extinction do
not deny the need for a new generation of crossbred

bananas: Once chromosome mutation has got you into a pickle, chromosome mutation is the only way out. But if you believe severely inbred varieties and GMOs pose a clear and present danger to the free world, you are sadly mistaken. The battle was lost a long time ago.

The history of Americans eating the forbidden fruit of the tree of knowledge began with the apple. In 1625 a Pilgrim named William Blaxton planted the New World's first orchard, and a few years later emerged the Blaxton's Yellow Sweeting. Thousands of newfangled American apple varieties followed, but only about one hundred have trickled down into present markets. Americans spend more than $1 billion each year on applesauce, apple juice, and raw apples, but before we get all misty-eyed about the number of home-baked apple pies gracing checkered tablecloths each year, remember that these are not your grandma's apples. Johnny Apple-seed (the evangelical vegetarian, whose real last name was Chapman) would not recognize the modern art of genetic markers and breeding gradients, nor could he have comprehended orchards of chemically engineered, chemically fertilized, and chemically pesticized apple trees, diligently monitored by teams of bioregulators. Despite nursery rhymes to the contrary, apples no longer grow from apple seeds—which include too much of that bothersome genetic variability. Commercial apples are cloned apples, and Johnny Appleseed's favorite, the tart green Rambo, has long been forgotten, completely

overwhelmed by the Red Delicious, which boasts
U.S. Plant Patent No. 2,816.

They are all patented. From nectarines and
peaches to carrots and artichokes, the fruits and
vegetables we consume are all someone else's intellectual property. As for the grains, the intricacies of
rice genetics, wheat genomics, and the creation of
ever more stress-tolerant soybean hybrids constitute not only a sizable chunk of the business conducted at the U.S. Department of Agriculture but a
glut of advanced research at institutes of higher
learning across the country. Two to four new wheats
emerge each year, copyrighted, ready to replicate,
raring to join the 1,199 mutant varieties of cereal
that already glut the market. And when it comes to
funding food tech, sorghum pathology laboratories
compete with peanut-breeding protocols and com-
puterized databases that model lentils, limas, and
garbanzos. The end result: In 2005 the National Science Foundation, the Department of Energy, and
the USDA pooled resources and awarded a $32 mil-
lion grant to sequence the corn genome.

Yet the most intricate chromosome patterns of
oats, peas, beans, and barley pale before that of a
single chicken. The complete and final fowl genome
has disclosed no less than a billion nucleotides,
which bind together the twenty-two thousand genes
of the domesticated rooster (roughly the same number of genes as necessary to formulate the domesticated human being, but in somewhat different order).
Although the world's chicken population may stand

threatened by avian flu virus, the revelation of the *Gallus gallus* genotype has presented numerous opportunities for breeders, and the USDA has moved ever deeper into its obsession with collecting and purveying poultry sperm (much of the commercial fowl industry relies exclusively on artificial insemination).

The National Center for Biotechnology Information (a subsidiary of the National Institutes of Health) has registered nearly a thousand chicken clones, and that is the merest beginning. Stores of cryopreserved chicken germplasm may one day inseminate millions of genetically identical eggs, which will roll off sterile production lines fifty thousand an hour and hatch into armies of replicate birds. The Platonic ideal of poultry would be the superchicken, a featherless biped that will mature faster than Perdue, taste better than free-range, never catch cold, and eat like a bird. (Already avian gene libraries have enabled chicken science to achieve victory over long-standing foes, like that funny smell in raw brown eggs.) At the end of the long conveyor belt that will constitute their life, the clucking carbon copies will not be shocked to find themselves custom gutted for the American stomach, from genetic wunderkind to shrink-wrapped breasts and thighs in a few dozen mechanized seconds.

The wild boar dates back to the Ice Age, and America's eight primal pigs landed with Columbus. A mere 350 years later, a visiting Englishman could describe Broadway as "six miles of roast pig!" Today, annual retail pork sales top $4 billion, and Monsanto's swine-genome project will soon provide the bioinformatics necessary to breed pigs for color, marbling, odor, flavor, juiciness, tenderness, and texture (not to mention meat pH, protein levels, calories, vitamins, minerals, and cholesterol). If approved, Monsanto's twelve pending pig patents will cover almost any pig, anywhere in the global pork chain. And you may wonder—what will Monsanto do once it owns the intellectual rights to every hog on earth?

Here is one guess: Even those remotely involved in the pig business know that the American stomach will not allow the American mind to purchase pale pork meat, a coloration that occurs as a result of porcine stress syndrome (PSS). The pig pros know that swine stress emerges from a recessive gene, so it will be a matter of some urgency for Monsanto (and its subsidiaries and partners, such as the Pig Improvement Company) to breed away every last peptide of that protein.

Perhaps a DNA injection will do the trick, or a mighty batch of microwaved porcine seed. Or simply trocar some high-performance hog serum into Porky's fetus as he lies unconscious in the womb. And if swine biotechnology can breed away pig fear of death, a rosy future may await the rest of us. The Pentagon would be quite interested in any kind of technology that could result in fearless humans. Imagine the applications. . . .

While we await a full uncoding of the death-stress gene in swine and men, we can still induce courage the old-fashioned American way: We can eat red meat. Each year the American stomach consumes 25 billion pounds of beef, to which we should add the portions of cattle carcass it refuses to consume (in 2003 Indonesia imported more than thirteen thousand tons of cow viscera from the United States—mostly for the Asian meatball market). The enormity of the beef business has created entirely new fields of research and development, and meat science has grown and prospered. Companies like Pyxis Genomics and Genaissance Pharmaceuticals specialize in genotyping cattle. If you need to clone a cow or purchase some Hereford gene software, if you're unsure about genetic markers or chromosome mutations, just put in a call to the U.S. Meat Animal Research Center in Clay Center, Nebraska. They can direct you to meat laboratories from Cal Poly Pomona to Iowa State, Michigan State, Oklahoma State, Texas A&M, and the University of Maryland, where a doctoral student named Jason Matheny recently outlined methods not for birthing and feeding and butchering beef but for growing the raw red tissue in long, thin, antiseptic sheets right there in the laboratory. Upton Sinclair would have been proud.

From the smallest grain of quinoa to the hugest side of cow, our food is not what it seems. Long ago it lost its innocence, and ever since it has been restructured, revamped, reconfigured, and reconstituted. And we shall continue to rebuild it, make it better than it was before. When it comes to consumption, Americans like to play God. And where the stomach leads, all else follows. No matter that we have devoured the old Eden of chestnuts, beechnuts, walnuts, and butternuts. No matter that Indian as it once was has been sequenced out of existence. We can create a new world and eat it, too.

Of course, genetically modified manna isn't quite the same as the original. Sometimes a little problem will arise. Here and there the stomach becomes frustrated. And then desperate. And then things can get ugly, scary, and extraordinarily complicated.

Consider the oyster. Since time immemorial the American stomach has been steeped in corruption, but only oyster sin qualifies as original, and only oyster sin provides a glimpse into the rapture. The final revelations of the American stomach may not deliver the thrills of bottomless pits, seven-headed dragons, or lakes of fire heaped with living dead. But it will include plenty of oyster sex-change operations.

In this country, oyster covetousness and oyster gluttony (more commonly described in the extensive oyster literature as oyster panics and oyster manias) go back a long way. Hundreds of years before the first peckish Puritan waded into the muddy shallows of Salem Bay and plucked an oyster as if it were a submerged strawberry, the Native Americans had been gorging. In 1634 colonist William Wood marveled at the oysters of Massachusetts Bay, which measured one foot in length:

> The fish without shell is so big, that it must admit of a division before you can well get it into your mouth.

Chief Massasoit courteously instructed the strangers with funny hats how to harvest the shellfish, how to steam them open, and how to cook them in stews. Without oysters the settlers would have starved. Perhaps they should have been grateful.

Second-generation Puritans could already sense that oysters augered profound and dire portents. The first environmental protection law ever ratified in this country was passed in 1679:

> To protect the destruction of oysters in South Bay, by the unlimited number of vessels employed in the same.

And oysters became central players in America's first litigation over private property, public waterways, and government regulation. For the growth of the colonies demanded ever more protective oyster legislation, and the Enlightenment bivalve soon expanded its political and economic clout. One of New York's early newspapers, *The Independent Re-*

flector, devoted an entire article in the fall of 1753 "to the honour of oysters," which "are serviceable both to our king and country":

> Some gentlemen, a few years ago, were at the pains of computing the value of this shell-fish to our province in general. The estimate was made with judgment and accuracy, and their computation amounted to ten thousand pounds per annum.

War could not kill them. After the British fleet seized New York Harbor and all its oysters in the torpid summer of 1779, food prices inflated 800 percent. Oyster prices spiked along with the political tensions, so the occupying forces fixed rates and set heavy fines for violators. A slave caught selling oysters above official valuations would receive his or her "punishment at the public whipping-post." General Putnam awarded oystermen special permits to stay in business, perhaps because the English were as obsessed with oysters as the colonials. To emulate the metallic piquancy of their native Colchesters, the redcoats seasoned their subjugated City Islanders and East Rivers with filings of copper. Copper is highly toxic, but if and when anyone began to vomit, it was always the oysters, never the oyster sauce, that served as a convenient scapegoat.

Considering the appetite of the Yankees and the English and that Miss Leslie's duck pies demanded "a quarter of a hundred oysters" each (and that native East Coast oysters are vulnerable to more lethal diseases than any other commercial mollusk, and particularly susceptible to parasites), it may come as no surprise that the native American oyster became our country's first extinction. Boston's Wellfleets and the primeval reefs of Cape Cod had both given out by 1775, and Staten Island's natural beds failed before the War of 1812. But these were petty inconveniences. The nouveau riche Jacksonian mobocracy still flocked to the gold carvings, mirrored arcades, damask curtains, and crystal chandeliers of Downing's, the poshest oyster parlor in Manhattan, where tycoons sucked down raws at a rate Dale Boone would have admired.

In 1830, just as Downing's hit unprecedented metabolic and economic success, something strange happened: Every last Long Island Bluepoint suddenly vanished from the Atlantic muck. To this day no one knows why. To this day no one has cared why. Perhaps it was the angel of death. Perhaps the hand of God. Instead of bothering with such imponderables, the watermen dumped boatloads of Chesapeakes into the Great South Bay and hoped they would not succumb. It took nine years before one of these newfangled, imported "Bluepoints" made it back to market, but the American stomach had demanded an oyster from the Long Island Sound, and it would have one.

A pattern had been set: rampant hysteria regarding the total elimination of a native oyster closely followed by maniacal imports of new species, which sometimes solved the problem, sometimes did not, and often created more problems than they solved. Soon after the California gold rush, San Francisco's delectable Pacific natives went bust. East Coast growers theorized that what had worked for the Long Island Bluepoint would work for the West Coast Olympia, so they shipped masses of their Chesapeake Bays across the country. But on their backs and deep within their guts the East Coast oysters carried East Coast protozoans, East Coast bacteria, East Coast viruses, and other various and sundry East Coast killers that still ravage shellfish from British Columbia to Newport Beach.

They come in all different sizes, shapes, tastes, and price points, but they are all the same. The Nova Scotian Chedabucto, the Rhode Island Moonstone, the Massachusetts Wellfleet, and the Long Island Bluepoint, indeed all of America's native oysters—from the St. Lawrence River to the bayous of Lake Pontchartrain and on down to the Atlantic coast of Argentina—constitute a single species, *Crassostrea virginica.*

When Captain John Smith sailed up the Chesapeake Bay in 1607, massive reefs of *virginica* threatened to rip the hulls of his three ships, and by the late 1880s the descendants of these colonial shellfish constituted the greatest oyster-producing region in the world. At its epic height, the Chesapeake

Bay's oyster industry employed one out of five Americans who worked in the fishing business, and yearly harvests exceeded 3 billion bivalves. Today the Chesapeake's share of the U.S. domestic oyster product has virtually vanished. The native eastern oyster—which *The Grocer's Encyclopedia* of 1911 called "one of the most democratic of food luxuries"—has been depleted to less than 1 percent of its abundance only thirty-five years ago. In other words, it's over.

But the demise of the storied East Coast oyster industry has a bearing distinct from all fiscal, Freudian, Foucauldian, New Historicist, Marxist, evangelical, and even culinary considerations. In order to survive, the Chesapeake Bay must process an astounding variety of nutrient and waste products through intricate webs of ingestion and excretion, and over thousands of years *virginica* has evolved as the central protagonist in this latticework of eating and being eaten. But now *virginica* is just about gone.

For thousands of years the oyster's digestive system had clarified and purified the bay's waters by functioning as its magical guts, delivering sun power to the deep by transmuting the energy of the plant life on which it feeds to the smallest finfish, which live on oyster larvae. But the steady degradation of the Atlantic coast's native eastern oyster over the past 150 years has occluded the Chesapeake Bay's natural circulations to the extent that it suffers from a massive case of dyspepsia. The Chesapeake may no longer be able to feed itself, much less support the needs of the bivalve business. This time the American stomach had really done it.

Some believe it is only a matter of time before the Chesapeake Bay—like the Cavendish banana—rolls over and dies. The first indication will be the death of the oysters, and they are already out the door. But there is one man determined to save the shellfish, save the business, save the bay, and make a profit: A man determined to replace *virginica* with something new, something better. Standish K. Allen is the latest in a long line of American scientists devoted to building a better oyster, a lineage that began in 1888 when Rutgers University appointed its first Professor of Biology and Its Applications in Developing Food Products. A decade later the state of New Jersey granted Rutgers $200 to establish an "Oyster Investigation Laboratory" somewhere in the sands of Cape May.

Standish K. Allen is a stocky man with a deep-lined, sunbaked face, and his wavy hair, streaked with gray, often falls across but never obscures the intensity of his light blue eyes. I stood beside him as the noonday sun bore down on the Chesapeake. "It's desperation down here," admitted Allen. "The shit has hit the fan."

The Chesapeake's devastated oyster harvests have ushered in nationwide increases in oyster imports, which ballooned 70 percent from 1994 to 2001, and jumped another 12 percent in 2003. The escalating figures outline a vast phenomenon: The largest contributors to the United States' trade deficit are oil and energy imports, but seafood imports hold the number two spot, accounting for a $7 billion chunk of the deficit. And so the federal government has come to consider aquaculture in general—and oyster husbandry in particular—to be in the national interest. Which may help to explain Stan Allen's record of federal oyster study grants, which have totaled more than $3 million since 2001.

Despite the seafood deficit in general and the catastrophic predicament of the East Coast oyster in particular, Stan Allen does see a lot of oysters. On a typical day he may review more than a hundred thousand, and when the real exotics come his way—a curious new batch of Korean bivalves, for example—Allen knows just what to do. In the long-standing tradition of American xenophobia, he will deposit the funky shelled foreigners in biosecure quarantine at the new, $1.4 million Kauffman Aquaculture Center, where the lab technicians shower and iodine wash in and out and wear long white plastic aprons and white rubber clogs.

The doors to the Kauffman Center remain locked at all times, the premises monitored by advanced alarm systems. A gigantic plastic liner underneath the brick building protects against any possible leakage of alien oyster or oyster pathogen. At the highest shellfish security tier, Level 1, the center features negative air pressure, HEPA filters, and ultraviolet purifiers for any water rereleased into the Chesapeake Bay. At Level 1 the Kauffman Aquaculture Center feels like a cross between Fort Knox and the secret lab in *The Andromeda Strain*.

Aside from the biosecure Kauffman Aquaculture Center, Standish K. Allen presides over a number of more traditional oyster hatcheries at the Virginia Institute of Marine Science (VIMS), where he is a professor of marine science. In the first few weeks of every summer for the past several years, Stan Allen has entered his temperature-modulated broodstock room, selected a number of custom-mutated Chinese oysters (*Crassostrea ariakensis*, as opposed to the Atlantic coast native, *Crassostrea virginica*), and carried them out to a lab table. Here, Allen slices the Asian oysters open, then lacerates their tissue and oyster eggs and oyster sperm fog together in a glass beaker. "The barbaric ritual of creating life," Allen calls it.

By the middle of June, Stan Allen had spawned more than a million of his own specially patented, custom-made oysters. These are the fulfillment of the long-standing gastrosophical fantasy: an invulnerable food, oversize and impervious to pollution and disease, a redemptive food, numb to any temptation other than keeping its own belly—and our bellies—full. A perfect food—except for the fact that it can never be kosher.

Tossed into the eddies and currents of the Chesapeake Bay, Stan Allen's newborn Asian bivalves would have swum and drifted hundreds of miles. Locked inside the biosecure premises of VIMS, more than a million of the microscopic larvae easily fit within the confines of a single fifty-gallon plastic tub. Here, Stan Allen's mutant Chinese brood circled until that day in early July when the professor and his summer crew of grad students and high school interns spiced the bouillabaisse with a shot of epinephrine, which excited the little dog paddlers to the point where they shook their cilia one last time and sunk to the bottom of the tank.

Instead of squirming larvae, the animals had become sedentary oysters. Soon afterward, as the spat gorged on increasing concentrations of antiseptic algae cooked up in the hatchery's air-conditioned kelp kitchen, they began to develop feathery shells. A few weeks hence, when the toddlers had grown to the length of half a fingernail, they would journey outdoors for the first time in their lives to a fenced-in, padlocked, high-security, percolating pond system.

It was here I found Standish K. Allen gazing into the plastic pools that seethed with his creations; but Stan was not happy. It was already late summer, past time for his million Asian superoysters to bid adieu to bioseclusion and drop into the Chesapeake. Many weeks past scheduled deployment and still the oysters had not grown large enough for the open water. Not only was the professor losing faith that any of his brood could reach the half-shell market by Christmas, he had, as they say, a legal obligation. Every nonnative oyster dropped into the bay had to be removed from the bay within a year. That was the deal: a million patented oysters in, a million patented oysters out. No oyster left behind.

Why not simply dump them in and leave them there? Why not let Stan Allen's Asian oysters thrive like Chesapeake Bays in the Long Island Sound or San Francisco Bay a century and a half before? Why not let them increase and multiply like patented strawberries, corn, and swine? The answer has less to do with digestion than it does with that other great involuntary impulse: not human sex, but oyster sex.

One of America's greatest living oyster-sex experts comes from China. His name is Ximing Guo, and he can trace his family tree back four hundred years in Dong Guang, the village of two thousand where he was born. Today Ximing Guo lives in New Jersey with his wife and two daughters. A professor of molluscan genetics and aquaculture at Rutgers's Harold Haskin Shellfish Research Laboratory, Guo was for many years Stan Allen's closest colleague.

Professor Guo explained that every oyster is born male, and that each little boy reaches sexual maturity on his first birthday, at which point he participates in what will become the annual rite of spring: choosing what gender to be for the next twelve months. Some oysters stay as they are, some decide to go female, while the indecisive bivalves (about one in fifty) will spend the upcoming year as hermaphrodites.

Guo pointed out that researchers and food technologists have been trying to figure out why oysters change sex, but none has met with success. There may be a compelling reason for an oyster, surrounded by ten thousand females, to become a man. Then again it might be advisable to go with the flow. Maybe it has something to do with waterborne pheromones. Maybe not. Although oyster sexperts can only theorize about how and why the animal decides its persuasion, the resolutions are not fatally binding. With the arrival of every spring, the oyster gets yet another opportunity to make up his or her mind—if an oyster has a mind . . . or just a brain in its gut.

Of course, the oyster's sexual liberation does nothing to gratify oyster gatherers, processers, retailers, ingesters, and the American economy. If an oyster elects to be male, during the summer breeding season it may devote up to 60 percent of its body's energy to developing oyster gonads, and while such a single-minded commitment may feel excellent to the adolescent oyster, it does nothing for the meat. As Professor Guo drily put it in one of his position papers, "Animals with excessive gonadal material cannot be marketed." A starving person could swallow one without harm, but a gonad-producing oyster looks rather strange on the half shell, and the egg-crammed female is rather mushy. The oyster—once all digestion—has become all procreation.

And so a great deal of federal money has been spent on creating something called the triploid oyster, an oyster that does not care about sex, an oyster made for human digestion and nothing else. And it is the pursuit of the triploid oyster that brings us back to the centuries-old American quest for the gastrosopher's stone: From Cotton Mather to Sylvester Graham, Benjamin Rush to William Beaumont, Catharine Beecher to Barry Sears, Benjamin Franklin to Standish K. Allen—our greatest minds have sought the magical property that could transmute the dross of the stomach depraved into digestive gold.

And so the manifestation of the triploid oyster may define the future of food, it may be an emblem of all to come. But what exactly is it?

One early afternoon at the Haskin Shellfish Research Laboratory, Professor Ximing Guo led me beyond the large orange and white AUTHORIZED PERSONNEL ONLY and BIOHAZARD signs and into his lab, where he and a crack team of oyster-molecule experts had created the world's first—if extremely partial—genetic map of an oyster. Dr. Guo clicked awake a computer screen, which displayed an oyster gene sequence, a line of code that began TAATGAACTTACTT and never came to an end.

"This is tedious work," he said, but in order to

understand what a triploid oyster means, one must understand oyster DNA. Guo explained that the oyster gene set is more than 30 percent identical to the human genome, which would mean that each of us is (roughly) one-third oyster. Guo told me that a few years back he had joined a consortium that proposed sending an oyster through human-genome sequencers, a project with a price tag of $50 million. The scheme did not receive funding. Building a better oyster may remain in our national interest, but federal genome-mapping priorities rank the oyster well below the catfish.

For the next three hours Guo told the tale of triploidy, drawing one extraordinary diagram after another on his small dryboard. I could not understand what the hell he was talking about. Not even a little bit. So we took a break.

There are 2½ restaurants in Bivalve, New Jersey, and the only place that offered table service was closed for the season, so we ended up at a joint on East Main Street called Dino's, which featured five Formica tables screwed into the wall. "I think it's unfortunate we don't have more funding for oyster genomics," Guo said as he examined the menu. "That is the key to building a better oyster."

Which was when Guo finally explained the triploid oyster in words that I could understand. Almost all animals, from human beings to sheep and scallops, are what geneticists call diploids, which means they possess two sets of chromosomes, one from Mom and one from Dad. A triploid, on the other hand, possesses three sets of chromosomes, a huge extra chunk of genetic protein lurking within every cell of the body.

America has long been enchanted by triploid fruit: Think seedless watermelons and seedless bananas (specifically that dwarf Cavendish dessert banana that may soon vanish from the face of the earth). Like these common, chromosome-mutated, man-made delicacies, a triploid oyster lacks seed. The extra chromosome has made it barren.

There are many benefits to a food that cannot enjoy sex, a food that has only eating on its mind, a food that is nothing but stomach. As Sylvester Graham had suspected a century and a half before, all of life came down to mastering the great twin involuntary passions: digestion and copulation. Graham had perceived the gathering storm clouds of gastro-porn and takeout sushi hovering above the American horizon, so he had preached a gospel of room-temperature mush. But it had taken Dr. Xi-ming Guo to transform such faith into practical power, to turn sexlessness into potency.

Dr. Guo was the first to theorize that since epicene oysters would expend no energy on their sexual development, they would develop a form of gigantism—which, for oyster sellers and eaters, is a very good thing. In addition to their uncanny ability to grow fast, grow big, and remain indifferent to anything but their next meal, triploid oysters may be more disease resistant than diploids; and because they are sterile, triploids will never produce gonads or eggs, so their meat can be brought to market any time of the year. Even in months without an R. And there is no difference in taste: The world's finest oyster connoisseur cannot differentiate a diploid from a triploid.

But what may be the most seductive attribute of the impotent oyster involves the introduction of an exotic species—such as Stan Allen's patented triploid Asian oyster, *Crassostrea ariakensis*—into American waters—such as the Chesapeake. Since the native oysters had gone bust, it was up to the nonnatives to save the Bay. Or utterly demolish it: And now that everyone understands the ecological ruination nonnative species portend, government regulators know to watch the bivalve business. (Thus the ultraviolet purifiers of Stan Allen's Level 1 biosecure oyster facility.) But if the alien oysters cannot have sex, if the alien oysters don't even *want* to have sex, slipping them into a new environment takes on a different complexion. Native populations may sicken and die en masse, but there are endless supplies of lab-baked Asian oysters. As long as they have been chromosomally castrated, foreigners do no harm.

Here, then, enteric outsourcing.

As a master's candidate at the University of Maine, Stan Allen became one of the first to attempt—and to fail—to create a triploid oyster. While pursuing his doctorate at the University of Washington,

Allen and yet another of his ex-colleagues, Sandra Downing, finally managed to produce a three-chromosome animal in the lab—and immediately filed the world's first patent application for a man-made higher life-form. Ultimately Allen and Downing did not win the intellectual rights to their first triploid oyster, but the decision denying them a patent has since become a legal landmark, the first judicial ruling that admitted the possibility of copyrighting chicken or beef. The door had been opened.

Ph.D. in hand, Dr. Stan Allen landed one of the top jobs in the oyster research world, a tenure-track appointment at the oldest molluscan study facility in America, the storied Harold Haskin Shellfish Research Laboratory in Bivalve, New Jersey. Here, Stan Allen turned his attention to the calamities of the East Coast oyster. He knew that hatcheries in Washington State had grown prosperous by creating and marketing millions upon millions of Japanese triploids (*Crassostrea gigas*), but in order to create the necessary sexual modification to the epicene beasties, workers had to dose the oyster spat with one substance called cytochalasin B and another called dimethyl sulfoxide. No problem, except for the fact that both chemicals are well-known and powerful carcinogens.

If you've eaten any oysters in the last quarter century or so, you've probably digested at least a few of these drugged beauties. No matter: Cytochalasin B and dimethyl sulfoxide cannot translate their poisons to the table-ready product on the half shell (not to mention the oysters in oyster bakes, oyster stuffings, or oyster stews). It's not the oyster eater at risk here but the oyster factory worker.

The American gut had finally met a worthy opponent: occupational-hazard litigation. But Stan Allen knew just what to do. He required tort-free triploids he could patent and sell, so he put in a call to the best oyster number cruncher he knew, a young Chinese postdoc by the name of Ximing Guo. Allen brought Guo to Rutgers, where the two faced a godlike challenge: not how to manufacture mutant oysters (that, they already knew), but how to manufacture the mommies and the daddies of the mutants—a feat no one had ever dared attempt.

It all came down to the number one—as in one more set of chromosomes. Allen and Guo knew that a mollusk with three sets of chromosomes could miraculously regain its lost sex drive with the addition of a fourth set of chromosomes. And the exquisite beauty of this purely hypothetical *tetraploid oyster* would be that when mated with normal, two-chromosome oysters, the oyster sperm and oyster eggs would naturally combine to produce hundreds of millions of triploid oyster babies. No carcinogens necessary—just good old-fashioned fornication. No occupational-hazard litigation possible. Big profits guaranteed. Of course, there was no such thing as a tetraploid oyster. It didn't exist anywhere but in the minds of Stan Allen and Ximing

Guo. And so the tetraploid oyster became the bivalve of their dreams.

Or so it seemed, until Allen and Guo discovered that it was virtually impossible to shove not one but two extra sets of chromosomes into the yolk of an oyster egg forty-millionths of a meter long. All they needed was a bigger oyster egg—but where to find one? After days and weeks of rumination, the partners finally hit upon the idea of cramming an additional set of chromosomes into the titanic ovum of one of their own carcinogenically produced triploid oysters, a specially selected überoyster, one with a serious case of oyster gigantism. Yet the triploid oyster was, by definition, sexless. Like the impotent banana and the seedless watermelon, a triploid would not produce any eggs, much less the gargantuan nucleus Allen and Guo fantasized.

But triploidy is not destiny. Despite the hype, triploids are not 100 percent barren. "One hundred percent is a physics thing," explained Stan Allen. "Not a biology thing."

Like Sarah, who presented Abraham with a son when she was ninety, the fruitless oyster can bear fruit after all. It is an improbable scenario: A three-chromosome oyster is about a millionth as likely to reproduce as a two-chromosome oyster. One in a million may be a lousy set of odds in horse racing or for getting into Yale, but it is statistically significant, particularly when it comes to the sweepstakes of the stomach.

So, for four years Stan Allen and Ximing Guo waited while technicians at the oyster research lab in New Jersey sliced open thousands upon thousands of triploids, searching for eggs. And since bivalve fertility cannot be detected by the naked eye, every gray ounce of raw oyster meat had to be scraped, sampled, and inspected under a dissecting microscope. Here was food research and development that would have made a mashgiach pale. No gastrosopher had ever conceived of such an intervention. But after countless failed trials, retooled techniques, and revamped hypotheses, there it was, the world's first tetraploid oyster. An oyster with not one but two extra sets of chromosomes. An oyster to befit this land of plenty. The oyster the American stomach had demanded.

Then the fear of mutant ninja oysters began to grow. After all, like everything else in biology, Allen and Guo's superoyster technology was not 100 percent effective. Their oyster sex orgies could guarantee 999 sterile shellfish out of each 1,000 produced, which seems like a good deal until you do the math: 999 out of 1,000 means that when Stan Allen's million mutant Asian triploids splash down in the Chesapeake Bay every summer, at least a thousand reproductive foreigners will be released. Since a single female oyster can broadcast up to 114 million eggs, one thousand fertile female oysters in the bay means 114 billion mutant Asian oyster eggs. Now imagine 114 billion mutant Asian oysters on the move, spreading like tentacles up and down the eastern seaboard. Imagine the nightmare of full-grown sci-fi mollusks, enormous as beach balls, engulfing small children as they frolic in the foam of South Beach and East Hampton.

And if Stan Allen's mutant oysters were called in to rescue America's oyster industry—which would not be a matter of 1 million Asian oysters dropped in the bay but 100 to 300 million Asian oysters in the bay—Allen and Guo would stand to sell 100 to 300 million of their patented sexless oyster spat, every year, year after year, for an intellectual property fee of a penny apiece. "A hundred years of degrading the Chesapeake Bay and now we've got a quick fix for it, which involves ignoring the native species and bringing in a new species," summarized Dennis Hedgecock, of the National Academy of Sciences panel on nonnative oysters in the Chesapeake Bay. He then noted that Stan Allen and Ximing Guo held the patent: "Some of the elements of the dark scenario are there. And I credit Stan with being totally up-front about them."

"There's a clear conflict of interest," Allen has said on the record. "And I'm in the fucking middle of it."

Woe to Stan Allen! Breeding and sterility and genetic manipulation caused no biggie for the raspberry and the apple, the strawberry and the swine, the enzyme and the cow. No one cared when the

USDA came up with hexaploid wheat. No one even noticed when they discovered the allotetraploid great-grandparents of the soybean. All we did was eat. But when it comes to dropping a billion foreign bivalves in the Chesapeake Bay, everybody goes berserk.

The first hundred thousand of Stan Allen's mutant oysters—the biggest and fattest of the experimental lot he had spawned in a beaker in early June—would finally hit the open water very late in the summer of 2006. As a favor to Stan Allen and to the Virginia Institute of Marine Science, Andy Drewer, president of the Virginia Seafood Council, was nurturing about four hundred thousand thumbnail-size baby bivalves in a primitive cinder-block shed on the eastern shore of Chesapeake Bay. Professor Allen dunked his hand into the thick silt of a plastic silo and brought up a muddy fistful of tiny shells. If this was the future of food, it did not look promising.

"They look pretty happy," Allen said.

He and his assistant hauled the perforated plastic silos out of the twenty-foot-long upwellers. Coated with a thick scum of green and black slime, the great rectangular colanders oozed dark liquid through screen bottoms and the discharge pooled on the shed's concrete floor. Like some twisted parody of Emeril or Bobby Flay, Stan Allen dipped a Tupperware measure into the first colander and began to count how many mud-slathered mollusks were in each liter. The shed was sweltering and he was soon sweating, soaked with salt water, his face splattered with muck.

"I feel like we're in the oyster version of a meth lab," he said as he punched the keys of a filthy calculator.

The craft of transplanting oysters dates back to the ancient Romans, who collected spat on wooden branches and dug ponds to home-grow their beloved Breton bivalves. Today aquaculture accounts for 95 percent of global oyster production, but Andy Drewer's methods were not too different from the ancients. He clipped his oyster floats to large wooden stakes sunk into the water. And as the new species settled into Starling Creek and came to rest no more than eight inches below the still surface, no one said a word.

Deep within a cold metal chamber, in the face of frigid winds blasting from two merciless industrial-strength, galvanized metal fans, Michael Garvey rummaged for what was left of a bushel of oysters he had purchased from a Virginia supplier named Tom's Cove Aquafarms. Garvey has managed New York's Grand Central Oyster Bar for a decade and spends a great deal of his time matching oysters with appropriate liquid accompaniments—a Nova Scotian Tatamagouche demands Sauternes, a Matinecock from Long Island calls for dark sherry, while a Hampton Bay requires sake. Garvey oversees the sale of $8,000 in half shells each day, but on this particular late afternoon he was determined to hunt down one last taste of tetraploid-triploid *ariakensis*, and knew that somewhere in that shadowy walk-in refrigerator dwelt the final remnants of Stan Allen's Million Oyster March.

"There it is," grunted Garvey as he hoisted a blue mesh bag. "I'll pull a few."

The oysters had not been marketed as "Artificially Inseminated Sterile Asian Imports, copyright held by Stan Allen and Ximing Guo." No, these went by the name of "Bogue's Bay," an appellation taken from waters about an hour's boat ride from Chincoteague Island in Virginia. While the speediest of this brood of test-case triploids had gone to market at ten months (and had been consumed in September), the oysters Garvey withdrew from cold storage were the laggards, having attained market size at fourteen months. This is an astonishing number. The Chesapeake native, *Crassostrea virginica*, must sit and filter water for at least two years before reaching market size, at which point almost all have succumbed to pollution and parasites.

"Amazing," said Garvey as he carried four of Stan Allen's Asian triploids to the Grand Central Oyster Bar's champion shucker, Luis Iglesias, who stood surrounded by heaps of iced Bluepoints, stockpiles of lemons, and vast assemblages of cocktail sauce. Iglesias, who jimmies oysters seven hours a day, did not give the federally funded bivalves a second glance before he rinsed and pried them open.

Michael Garvey conducted the glistening half shells to a quiet counter spot for closer examination. "I can tell it will not be very creamy," he said, indicating the thin membrane that many oyster epicures prize. He gently poked one of the ninja oysters, none of which looked particularly threatening. "It's firm," said Garvey. "It looks like a very healthy oyster. Not plump, not thin, not dry. Plenty of juice."

He downed it straight.

"Very nice salinity, but not briny," he noted. "I get a spine of sweetness." He scrutinized the sparkling striations of the shell. "They didn't have a rough time at all."

Like Michael Garvey, Sandy Ingber, the Grand Central Oyster Bar's executive chef, had never heard of Allen and Guo's new tetraploid-triploid technology, but his reaction to the method was swift and unequivocal: "If there's more oysters for me to buy, and they're healthy and they're certified by the FDA, I say bravo. As long as they bring back the industry, I'm absolutely in favor." Moreover, the chef believes the "Bogue's Bay" Asian triploid favorably compares to the Belon, the world-famous European species originally harvested off France's Brittany coast, the oyster the Romans hauled in snow-packed carts to the banquet halls of their ancient capitol.

And what if customers were informed that Virginia's quaint "Bogue's Bay" was actually fronting for a Chinese river species that had been chromosomally whacked into existence by a laboratory in southern New Jersey? "That's what marketing is all about," said Ingber. "If and when you get approval, bring in the PR people. We have another triploid on our menu, the Westcott Bay Sweet from the San Juan Islands. A wonderful oyster. I sell sixty dozen a week."

And so the oyster has become an imaginary creature, bearing not the least molecular resemblance to the archaic delights Powhatan and John Smith once savored, or to the roasteds Massasoit offered the Pilgrims at that first Thanksgiving feast. The American stomach had once been traumatized by the abundance of the water and the land, but now it was the other way around. Of course, it was in no one's best interest to broadcast such a fact. Despite the high-tech triploids, despite the imported Australians and Asians and the transplanted and crossbred parasite-resistant strains, Grand Central Oyster Bar management understands that in order to retail their product, fragility and scarcity must come across as vigorous plenty. And Michael Garvey knows he sells an imaginary oyster, savage, raw, and absolutely authentic, the primal rough-and-ready edible, fit only for those who have mastered their own essential connection with the vital forces of nature.

Today, for the first time in Grand Central Oyster Bar history, the name of an Australian-seed variety (brought into being by tetraploid technology in Washington State) has been written in chalk on the menu board. With a fresh, cucumbery finish, this was a gorgeous flower of an oyster, its shell resolving in slender, rippling crescents. But someone who could not resist alliteration had the temerity to dub it the "Tasmanian Triploid," and Michael Garvey was not at all pleased. "I want to know who lettered it," he declared, "and I'm going to find out. Carlos!" he called. "Who wrote that 'Tasmanian Triploid'?"

"David," murmured a waiter.

A few moments later the general manager obliterated ontogeny, replaced it with geography, and the "Tasmanian Triploid" became the "Tasmanian Totten Inlet"—a reference to the renowned, bivalve-rich estuary of southern Puget Sound. But as the lunchtime roar of the Oyster Bar reached a crescendo, I could hardly hear Michael Garvey. I nodded anyway and gazed at the tables. Everywhere someone was sucking down an oyster—or at the very least something that looked and smelled and tasted like one.

1

Gut Reaction

But his horror was still more increased on observing that the head, which should have rested on his shoulders, was carried before him on the pommel of the saddle.

—Washington Irving,
"The Legend of Sleepy Hollow"

Yet another Thanksgiving Day was approaching, another year of the American stomach come and gone. Despite my objections, Lizzie had decreed that this short history required an annual pilgrimage north, to the pewter plates and pottage of the Plymouth harvest dinner reenactment. She had made reservations for the five of us, which included nine-year-old Phoebe, six-year-old Julian, and Grammy.

We spent the afternoon wandering hut to hut at the reconstructed Puritan "Plantation," then hiked a quarter mile to the "Indian" encampment, where the children huddled around the campfires and gaped at the sullen faces of the native reenactors. As darkness fell we filed inside the main building, past security and the souvenir shop, and settled at long tables beneath fluorescent track lights.

"What's for dinner?" asked Julian.

I studied the self-consciously old-fashioned orthography of the xeroxed menu: ciderkin, sallet, stewed pompion.

"Pumpkin," I said. "You'll like it."

In his *History of New York*, Washington Irving chronicled that after the crafty English settlers successfully executed a surprise attack against a Dutch stronghold in Connecticut,

> a strong garrison was immediately established . . . consisting of twenty long sided, hard fisted Yankees; with Weathersfield onions stuck in their hats, by way of cockades and feathers—long rusty fowling pieces for muskets—hasty pudding, dumb fish, pork and molasses for stores; and a huge pumpkin was hoisted on the end of a pole, as a standard—liberty caps not having as yet come into fashion.

A pumpkin was the first Yankee flag. One hundred years before the Stars and Stripes, there was a squash.

As the Dutch and the English girded themselves for supremacy on the new continent, pumpkins became propaganda. At the Yankee grand council of the east, the Dutch had to endure the calumny of being labeled a race of mere cannibals and anthropophagi, inasmuch as they never eat cod-fish on saturdays, devoured swine's flesh without molasses, and held pumpkins in utter contempt.

While Dutch anti-pumpkinites accused the Yankees of being a

squatting, bundling, guessing, questioning, swapping, pumpkin-eating . . . crew.

But Washington Irving's political satire paled beside the symbolism of his world-famous squash-centric ghost story, "The Legend of Sleepy Hollow." When the itinerant schoolteacher, poetaster, and rejected suitor Ichabod Crane finally faced the headless horseman, the horrifying apparition held his detached cranium—a pumpkin, of course—before him on the saddle, directly in front of his ghostly gut. And when heads collided at the climax, the pumpkin trumped the brain.

Of all the vegetables mentioned in "Sleepy Hollow," the

yellow pumpkins . . . turning up their fair round bellies to the sun

most definitely recalled the human stomach.

And so I had delved deep into the natural history of the native American squash, emblem of the enteric brain. I had followed its horticultural development to the present. But I did not dare utter the words "pumpkin ploidy," nor recite the strange saga of transgenic and triploid pumpkins, hybrids and clones and polymorphic endosperm. I knew no one at the long table of the harvest dinner reenactment could have cared how many thirds of our genome we shared with the pumpkin, and no one was interested in the academic conferences or courses in pumpkin management offered by the University of Georgia.

After corn and oysters and apples and hot dogs, could there be a food more American than the pumpkin?

I had spent hours reviewing pumpkin economics and could have explained that pumpkin business is big business: Libby's, Nestlé's wholly owned subsidiary, canned 85 percent of the world's orange meat, most of it harvested within ninety miles of Peoria, Illinois. In 2006 pumpkin production topped out at 1.1 billion pounds.

I had studied the culinary deployment of the squash: Around this time of year pumpkin recipes abounded, and I had recently scrutinized ingredient lists for pumpkin pancakes, pumpkin mole, pumpkin flan, pumpkin profiteroles, and pumpkin Parmesan risotto.

I had even examined the social elements of pumpkin mania and could have told the story of the dedicated pumpkin hobbyist who had watered and manured an Atlantic Giant until it weighed more than thirteen hundred pounds. A world record.

I could have explained why pumpkins are kosher.

In fact, I had strived mightily to fit pumpkins into my history of the American stomach—but could not. I thought I had finished with them, but here they were. They had followed me to the Plymouth harvest dinner reenactment.

I gazed at the faux congregationalists in ruffles and flounce, tinfoil scabbards, and strung-out, scraggly hair. These Puritans were professionals, and when they lined up to introduce themselves, the hungry and increasingly cantankerous crowd of heritage eaters fell silent. Next thing we knew the troupe had launched into a scarily well-rehearsed benediction—

Grant us peace, GOOD LORD, that we use these meats REVERENTIALLY . . .

Between the turkey sauc'd and mussels seeth'd, the cabbage boil'd and pork roast'd, the Cotton Mather impersonators harmoniz'd and frolick'd. In the bad old days such unseemly and odious mirth during dinner would have earned an official censure. Real Puritans would have thrown the ensemble into the snow, drawn and quartered the blasphemers, or at the very least banished them to Rhode Island.

My punishment fantasies crashed before the long-awaited platter of stewed pompion, which we dutifully passed around the table. I spooned some of the dense mash onto my plate and examined the thick yellow paste, flecked with black. I brought a bite to my mouth and swallowed, but the bolus lodged itself in my esophagus and would not move.

"It needs some brown sugar," said Grammy.

"I think it's a texture problem," said Lizzie. "It needs eggs and cream."

"It needs chicken broth," said Grammy. "And it needs to be whipped up."

"This pumpkin is the worst thing in the world," said Phoebe.

"Can we leave?" asked Julian.

Soon, I promised.

I surveyed the swilling, swallowing, autofocusing crowd. No natives among us, and I wondered how many of the tribe remained in the woods, waxing bitter as they jumped from one moccasin to the next, anything to keep themselves warm around the dwindling smolders of twigs and leaves. It had grown very dark very fast, and in the distance I heard drums.

Here, among the steam trays and track lights, no one had bothered to clear the plates or platters, which lay burdened with the uneaten. Harvest dinner had finally come to an end, the stewed pumpkin congealed into pounds of gaudy spackle, and there would be no dessert. Everybody in the building knew we had suspended disbelief long enough, and as the children's eyelids drooped, grown-ups gulped the dregs of Bud Light or Shiraz and instinctively prepared to maneuver out the door, into the parking lot, onto the road, and back to bed—a routine as sure and certain as dinner down the alimentary canal, decline and fall.

But just as we were about to abandon our plastic chairs, the rent-a-Pilgrims blocked the exits.

"We thank thee heartily, Jehovah," they began in unison, and at these words of praise everybody rose, silent and satiate. I gazed upon the landscape of overheated faces and bulging guts, crinkled skin and yellowed eyes. I heard the actor-priests intone the final hymn, and watched two hundred food tourists bow their melon heads in peristaltic prayer. And when the assembly murmured a language as ancient as their viscera, I knew that Lizzie had been right. There was an excellent reason to be here: This was the end of the trail.

In the car going home everyone fell asleep, but my autonomic heart pumped like Ichabod's as he watched the headless horseman grasp the pumpkin, lift it high into the air, and take aim. The road was getting hard to follow, winding like an esophagus, and I felt the ancient gut terror of being lost in the wilderness. And then the pumpkin hit me in the head.

American religion, American economics, American politics, and American media had all been devoured by the great maw. At the Plymouth harvest dinner reenactment, where nothing was real except the food, the primal, eldest origins of this country had met the American stomach and gone down the hatch, too. And still, the enteric brain pushed forward. It wanted more.

So this is the way the world ends: Not with a bang but a belch.

ACKNOWLEDGMENTS

Emerson once wrote, "The greatest genius is the most indebted man." Taking "genius" out of the equation, I am most indebted to: Bonnie Nadell, who had the insight; Andrea Schulz, who figured it out; Luke Mitchell, for the big picture; Elizabeth Beier, for the details; Lewis Lapham, M Mark, Susan Morrison, Darra Goldstein, Melissa Harris, Jocelyn Zuckerman, and Ruth Reichl, for assigning a different kind of article; David Reynolds, Rebecca Mead, Arnold Kantrowitz, Matthew Greenfield, Nina Planck, George Prochnik, Molly Jong-Fast, Maryann Feola, Peggy Davis, Marcy Granata, Michael Hirschorn, John Ho, Cate Marvin, Andrew Leigh, and Wayne Koestenbaum, for excellent advice; Michael Congrove, Barbara Nitke, Sara Moulton, Stan Allen, Greg DeBrosse, Bob Tuschman, and Michael Garvey, for hospitality and conversation; Jonathan Deutsch, for introducing me to the academic world of foodways; Richard Drake, who twenty-five years ago thought he perceived some dementia; my parents, Millard and Lorraine Kaufman, for their unending support; Phoebe and Julian, for helping to keep it all in perspective; and Liz Berger, who deserves all of the credit (and none of the blame) for turning a gastric Luddite into a gastrosophisticate.

INDEX

Index

Index

Index

Index

Index

Index

Index

witches, 37–38, 46, 56
Wood, William, 160
woodchuck, 107

Yahweh, 37, 47, 80, 124, 149
"Yankee Doodle," 97–98
yeast, 74

yellow fever, 55
yogurt, 10

Zagat, 4
Zone Diet, 117, 119, 140, 141,
  144
Zoroastrianism, 71–72